Head On

Head On

How to Approach
Difficult Conversations Directly

Janel Anderson, PhD

GALE HOUSE

Head On: How to Approach Difficult Conversations Directly

Copyright © 2018 Janel Anderson

Quantity Sales. Special discounts are available on quantity purchases by corporations, associations, educational institutions, or promotional use. For details, please contact the author.

While efforts have been made to verify information contained in this book, neither the author nor the publisher assumes any responsibility for errors, inaccuracies or omissions.

The reader of this publication assumes responsibility for the use of the information. The author and publisher assume no responsibility or liability whatsoever on the behalf of the reader of this publication.

For worldwide distribution. Printed in the U.S.A.

Library of Congress Cataloging-in-Publication Data

Anderson, Janel K.

Head on: How to approach difficult conversations directly

ISBN-13: 978-0-9995809-1-2

1.   Business Communication

GALE HOUSE

For Andrew, Jocelyn, and Blake—

*who have taught me more about myself and life
than they could ever know.*

Contents

Part 2
Difficult Conversations: Step by Step

Part 3
Difficult Conversations in Context

Contents

Head On

Introduction

Here's a secret, the product of my research, observations, and experience: difficult conversations are made, not born. Even the least acrimonious discussion can *become* difficult when one person makes another defensive.

When that happens, conversation shuts down. Someone on the defense can't listen or reason well. It's not his fault; it's a physiological fact. Here's the scientific explanation: when someone is under attack, the body diverts blood and oxygen away from the neocortex. That's the part of the brain that performs logical reasoning, and it all but shuts down. Where do these precious resources go instead? The arms and legs. To help that person either throw punches or run. You know: fight or flight.

When you start a conversation by making the other person defensive, it's hard to reach agreement. And it's darn near impossible to actually come up with a creative or innovative solution.

But there's hope. I've developed a process for starting and staying with a conversation that has the potential to be difficult—in a way that doesn't make your partner want to put up their dukes or flee the room. I've been training people in this process for years.

They always ask if there's a book to take home, to consult, to continue helping them through these challenging—and undeniable—conversations.

And now there is.

WHAT'S THE SECRET?

Fear and anxiety significantly influence our interpersonal communication at work, whether we want them to or not. Difficult conversations are fraught with these emotions, which in turn, prohibit us from being fully aware and present in those conversations. In those difficult situations, if fear and anxiety run the show, we lose the ability to regulate our thoughts and emotions. Instead, we react. And we react defensively. Most often, these very conversations are the ones in which we most need to be fully aware and present.

What if there were another way? What if you had a method for holding a conversation in a manner that kept defensiveness at bay? Imagine a conversation on a difficult topic with a coworker or a family member in which neither party got defensive. A conversation in which neither party was provoked to defend her position or protect his self-concept. This book offers just such a method.

The result? Both partners can bring their best listening and critical thinking skills to the table. No one gets upset. Each person begins to understand the other person's position and perspective, even if they don't necessarily agree with them. They also start to see who else is affected by the situation. And finally, they reach agreement, or at least understanding.

This book provides exactly such a process, a process you can begin using in your very next conversation on a difficult topic.

THE SKILLS YOU WILL LEARN

The book is divided into three sections. In the first section, you will come to understand why we get defensive in the first place. This section, Communication and the Brain, takes a close look at what is happening in the brain when we feel threatened and how we are biologically wired to defend ourselves when we encounter threat. Chapter 1 examines what happens in our brains when we face threatening situations and how that directly influences our ability to communicate clearly and effectively with others. Chapter 2 explores stress and the degree to which it supports or inhibits our ability to discuss difficult topics. In Chapter 3 you'll come to know some of the major regions of the brain and how each of them plays a role leading up to and during difficult conversations.

The second section of the book specifically describes a step-by-step method for holding conversations on difficult topics, both when you initiate them and when they find you. This section, *Difficult Conversations, Step by Step*, provides a recipe of discrete, proven steps to follow when conducting the conversation. Chapter 4 goes over the first step in the process: preparing for the conversation, but not in the ways you might typically prepare. Instead, this chapter offers guidance on how to ready yourself emotionally for the conversation—even when someone else starts it. Chapter 5 covers the critical first steps in how you begin the conversation and offers a process for opening the conversation in a manner that is specifically designed to lower the other person's defenses.

Chapter 6 offers a technique for staying present in the conversation and dynamically responding to the other person so they feel heard and acknowledged. Chapter 7 prompts you to get curious and stay curious throughout the conversation. It encourages you to think more expansively about who is affected by the situation. And Chapter 8 helps you reach agreement even when agreement is hard to come by. It also addresses the inevitability that sometimes we aren't able to reach agreement, and explains how to close those conversations with the relationship intact.

The third section, Difficult Conversations in Context, applies the content from the first two sections to specific situations in work life. Chapter 9 addresses holding difficult conversations with your teams and how to approach problematic issues as they arise in meetings. In Chapter 10, you will learn how to handle awkward and difficult situations as they occur with colleagues in common areas such by the copier or in the cafeteria. Chapter 11 provides guidance on facilitating your annual performance review as well as incorporating feedback throughout the year for continuous improvement. Chapter 12 examines difficult conversations with senior leaders.

Finally, Chapter 13 concludes with a discussion on how to drive lasting cultural change, so that confronting difficult situations in organizations head on becomes commonplace.

A WORD ABOUT EXAMPLES

I provide a lot of stories throughout this book to illustrate the points I'm making and to demonstrate the concepts and techniques in action. In the years I've been doing this work, I've trained, given speeches, coached, and facilitated meetings for literally tens of thousands of people. I've heard stories that may sound very similar to your experiences. Other stories may surprise you, amaze you, or be drastically different from your experience. I use some of those stories in this book.

The stories come to me in side conversations with participants at training programs I deliver, in the hallway with audience members after keynote speeches I give, on the phone with coaching clients, and in prep calls and debriefs with executives when I facilitate meetings. My audience has been very generous with me in sharing their stories, sometimes seeking help or support or to get my reaction, and other times to share their triumphs in navigating difficult situations. Whatever the reason, I am indebted to my audience members for trusting me with their stories.

All of the stories in this book are true. Aside from changing the names and surface details to protect the privacy of those who have shared their stories with me, I share the stories as they came to me. The examples come directly from people like you, facing workplace and personal issues that are sometimes mundane, sometimes awful, and many, many more, somewhere in between.

HOW TO USE THIS BOOK

I encourage you to *do* this book. Naturally, you will read it but I challenge you to take it a step further and to *experience* the book, in addition to reading it. Use *Head On* as a guidebook for understanding what happens in the brain when fear and anxiety are present—for both you and your co-workers—and how that distorts communication and relationships at work. And then do something about it. Actively use the techniques and methods in the book to get different results than you have gotten before.

Each chapter concludes with a pair of exercises to help you implement what you learned. To take your practical learning further, there is a companion volume to this book called *The Head On Handbook*. There you will find many more exercises, checklists, and activities that will help you apply what you learn in this book to real situations you face in the workplace.

If you really use the resources in this book—no, *when* you do—you will develop a much higher degree of self-awareness (even if you are already highly self-aware!) that will, in turn, lead to better emotional regulation and enable you to achieve better overall outcomes in conversations on challenging topics and not-so-challenging topics too.

And as you will discover, they don't need to be "difficult conversations." Rather, they can be conversations that happen to be on challenging or difficult topics. The topic may remain difficult, but the conversation doesn't have to be.

In short, when a conversation makes its participants feel anxious, the clear and rational thinking that can help to address the situation head on is more difficult to access. You are about to discover how to get more of that clear, rational thinking in conversations on challenging topics, both from yourself and others.

Part 1

Communication and the Brain

CHAPTER 1

Fight or Flight

Shawn arrived to work on Thursday like any other Thursday. He managed by walking around, checking in with his team members who were already at their desks, saying hello to the office manager and heading to his office to check email and prepare for his morning meetings. He was a bit surprised to see a meeting invitation in his inbox for a meeting with his manager's boss, Mike, the vice president of the division. Meeting topic: Project Work. "That's odd," thought Shawn. He wasn't accustomed to getting project assignments from Mike.

He had ten minutes until the meeting so he swung by his manager's office to see if he might glean some information. The office was empty. Shawn started to get a sinking feeling in the pit of his stomach. He'd heard rumors of layoffs that were being announced this week. Most of those affected were in the New York office, or so the rumor went. But now he began to wonder if he would be among the fallen.

The ten minutes crawled by. Shawn took the elevator to the third floor and walked the very long hallway to Mike's office. When he arrived, Mike and Jasmine, from human resources, greeted him. There was a large, white envelope on the desk with Shawn's name on it. The sinking feeling he'd felt in his stomach earlier was gone. Now it felt like his stomach had completely dropped out of his body. His mouth was a desert wasteland, not a drop of moisture to be found. He swallowed hard and said hello.

"I'm sorry to be the one to deliver the news," Mike began. "As you know, the company is making some changes in our business model, based on the economy." Shawn struggled to hear the rest of what Mike said. A deafening sound thundered through Shawn's head. It sounded like the roar of a locomotive. He literally couldn't hear. He blinked and squinted, trying to focus on what was being said.

"It's all spelled out in the letter and the additional materials in the envelope," Jasmine explained. "Do you have any questions that we can answer right now?"

"My team," Shawn stammered. "My team. Do they know? Are they affected?"

"There's a meeting at eleven o'clock this morning with your team. They'll stay on. They'll be reporting to Jennifer starting next week. They'll have this week to wrap up the projects they've been working on with you and your clients," Mike explained.

Shawn took the envelope and walked to the door. His knees felt unsteady, his eyes blinked frequently and the sound of the locomotive still flooded his head, blocking all other sound. He passed by the elevator and took the deserted stairwell instead. The sound of his wingtips on the stairs echoed in the cement stairwell, and he could faintly hear the echo amidst the roar of the sound in his head. As he continued to his office, he wished more than anything that he could hide, not show up at the meeting with his team in two hours. If only he could disappear.

Shawn was experiencing classic symptoms of the sympathetic nervous system in his body. This chapter examines the impacts the sympathetic nervous system has on our bodies and can, in turn, have on interpersonal communication at work. In Shawn's case the additional blood flow away from his brain to his limbs accounted for the roar of the locomotive in his head and his difficulty hearing. His body was mobilizing for fight or flight. The blood that normally circulated to his brain for critical thinking, listening, and other cognitive tasks was rushing to his limbs to help him either fight off his attackers or run for his life.

From an evolutionary biology perspective, that's what our body is programmed to do: protect us by escaping from threats we are not able to easily fight off. Modern work activities typically are not ones we must fight (with our bodies) for our livelihood, nor are they the stuff we typically must run fast and climb a tree to safely escape from. Although it sometimes feels that way!

The evolution of work and life has occurred much more rapidly than our brains and bodies have evolved. We are still programmed to use our physical strength to fight and defend ourselves or run for our lives, escaping from threats at all costs. Our bodies do not distinguish between modern office politics and a saber-toothed tiger chasing us down. The body mobilizes quickly to escape the threat and does not slow down to critically examine the particulars of the situation. Our ancestors did not pause to thoughtfully consider what they would taste like when the tiger caught them. No, they ran for their lives and climbed that tree as fast as they could!

Likewise, we do not carefully consider the details and subtle nuances of our situation when the sympathetic nervous system is fully engaged and we are in full on fight or flight. We are programmed to find safety. Shawn's only refuge for the time being was his office. He wanted to flee, but he had just enough rational thinking to override his desire to leave the building.

Another person's response might have been different. Another person may have been argumentative and combative if they responded with the "fight" nature of the sympathetic nervous system. Others still might freeze up and find their ability to move, no less ask pertinent questions, to be completely incapacitated.*

The sympathetic nervous system, often referred to by its nickname "fight or flight," governs our reaction to threats, real and perceived. The emphasis for us is on *perceived*: since our brains and bodies have not evolved as rapidly as our modern environment, they get a lot of false positives in the "run for your life" category. That is, the body reacts as if the boss's explosion *du jour* is an actual threat to our survival—and whether you gear up to fight or shut down in flight, your boss will probably respond in turn.

Fight in the workplace shows up as yelling and screaming at staff and co-workers. It shows up as bullying and passive-aggressive behavior. It shows up as fierce competition for resources. It shows up as cc-ing your peers in an email accusing a co-worker of botching a project. And at its worst, it shows up as violence—from verbal attacks to punches thrown.

Flight, on the other hand, may show up as a literal physical departure (i.e., leaving the room) or as checking out and becoming less engaged. Flight, while seeming more innocuous than fight, significantly impacts individual relationships and organizational outcomes. When interpersonal communication between managers and employees is strained or dysfunctional, the resulting literal flight can cost millions of dollars in turnover. Remaining on the job while "checked out" may be costing organizations even more. Recent reports estimate the active disengagement of American workers results in an annual loss of $350 billion.[1]

_____

*For an excellent discussion of all the possible responses to threat, I recommend reading *Extreme Fear: The Science of Your Mind in Danger* by Jeff Wise.

Another reaction to fear is the freeze response. The freeze response is produced by the same part of the brain that generates both fight and flight. It is a response that no longer suits our environment, at least at work. When a manager, for example, puts an employee on the spot, stunning him or her to the point of no response, that's freeze. Standing utterly still may have helped our ancestors to avoid detection, but it's not very effective or professional in the concrete jungle.

YOUR BRAIN ON THREAT

As Shawn's example above demonstrates, a brain experiencing "threat" is not working at its best. When the brain is running an "escape threat" program, it will not be doing its optimal, clearest thinking. Rather, it will be seeking self-preservation and protection. In short, it is operating out of pure defensiveness. Think of the most recent time you were talking with someone who was feeling defensive. Whether it was a co-worker, a client, or your teenager, the threat—real or perceived—got in the way of them doing their best thinking, listening, and participating in the conversation.

Interpersonal Threat

Long before the recent breakthroughs in neuroscience, communication researchers were observing and documenting the causes and effects of defensiveness in communication. Chief among the early researchers was Jack Gibb. Dr. Gibb's work in the 1960s and 1970s at the University of Colorado, where he directed the Group Process

Laboratory, is critical to our current understanding of how defensive communication comes about. [2]

Gibb and other researchers found that defensiveness is sometimes caused by intolerance of those who hold different views. When we encounter views or beliefs that are different from our own, the juxtaposition of holding those two viewpoints simultaneously results in cognitive dissonance, or a set of incompatible perspectives, which can easily lead to defensiveness. In sum, when we encounter new information that is contrary to our present thoughts, feelings or beliefs, it may result instinctually in a fear that we may have to change those thoughts, feelings, or beliefs.

Researchers in the field of interpersonal communication have also been studying this phenomenon for decades. Dr. Anita Vangelisti at the University of Texas, Austin and a team of other researchers have found that defensiveness is predicated on a cycle of self-awareness of a flaw or inconsistency in oneself and a refusal to admit or acknowledge it. For example, if a person is inconsistent with how they handle money and their spouse wants to have a conversation about financial matters, the person may get defensive almost immediately at the start of the conversation. Additionally, the person experiences an accompanying sensitivity to the issue and easily perceives an attack on that area by another person, whether or not it is real. [3]

Defensiveness Begets Defensiveness

Neuroscience research focusing on mirror neurons demonstrates how easily we are influenced by other people's words and actions. In functional magnetic resonance imaging (fMRI) studies, researchers have found that when one person sees another individual performing an action, the same part of the observer's brain that is required to perform that action is activated, even though it is the other person who is performing the action.[4] So it is not surprising then that when one person acts defensive, the other person is likely to get defensive, too.

Throughout this section of the book, we are going to be discussing some of the parts of the brain that have a direct influence on communications and how they are related to our emotions. Keep in mind, though, that our human brains are extremely complex and handle many different kinds of processes, from remembering birthdays to dancing the Funky Chicken.

Additional research has shown that the defensive response is generated by the limbic system—the emotional part of the brain—before the neocortex—the rational part of the brain—is activated and has a chance to respond to the threat. When you form an initial perception of a situation, information that seems threatening is handled directly by the amygdala, part of the limbic system and the center of your fight or flight response. It bypasses the neocortex where critical thinking and listening occur.

For example, if your boss's boss sees you in the hallway and says rather sternly, "I need to see you in my office in five minutes," there is a good chance that your body will automatically react to this as a threatening situation. Your heart may begin to race or you may break out into a cold sweat, whether or not there is indeed a real threat. The information, including the verbal message and the nonverbal cues that accompany its delivery, gets passed directly to the amygdala before the neocortex can even get a chance to consider whether there is a real basis for a threat.

This bypass is designed for our survival. The human brain is conditioned to protect the body it inhabits. When there is a perceived threat, alarms are sent immediately to the body to mobilize and defend or to get out of harm's way quickly. That bypass, de-signed for efficiency, may not serve us well at the office, but it just may be responsible for our species still roaming the earth.

Breaking the Cycle

With the amygdala jumping into action in a threatening moment, how do you stand a chance at acknowledging the perceived threat and then examining that threat through the lens of the executive function of the brain? If you can manage to do it, you'll get an op-portunity to apply critical thinking skills to the situation. Then you can evaluate the perceived threat to determine the best course of action to take, given your desired outcomes.

This requires conscious and deliberate effort. It requires slow-ing down and interrupting the stimulus-response cycle which gov-erns our bodies and brains in potentially threatening situations. To do so requires an intimate and conscious awareness of how threat feels in our bodies. We each react somewhat differently to threat. To some it feels like a punch in the gut, to others it may feel like the oxygen has been sucked from the room. Still others will get a racing heartbeat or sweaty palms. And some may react like Shawn from the beginning of the chapter, with the deafening sound of a locomo-tive roaring through their heads. For most of us, it will vary from one situation to the next.

Take a minute now to reflect on a time when you felt threat-ened. Recall the experience with as many of your five senses as you can. Then, scan your body from head to toe and notice any and all sensations. Bringing your conscious awareness to these sensations will enable you to identify them more readily in situations of per-ceived or real threat. When you sense your body reacting, you will be more able to rationally evaluate situations that initially show up as threatening. You will be more able to head off false positives, making it more likely that what you say and do next is, in fact, informed by your rational brain and not by an unchecked, instinctive response to a threat.

EVOLUTIONARY BIOLOGY AND WORK CULTURE

The modern workplace has evolved much faster than our brains and bodies. You don't have to look farther than your boss sending you an email that says simply, "See me," to strike fear into the minds and bodies of most people. Our brain senses ambiguity in this message. Without knowing the valence of the message, that is, whether the message is a positive message or a negative message, the instinctive brain will default to interpreting it as a negative message. This is by design. Here's how it works:

When we encounter ambiguity around a particular situation and don't know if it is negative or positive, our amygdala first perceives the situation as negative or threatening as a protective measure. Assuming the worst can protect us from a possible threat. Threats, as we have already discussed, generate defensiveness.

From an evolutionary biology standpoint, our brains and bodies have a long way to go to catch up with the changes in the modern workplace. It is in our DNA to feel defensive when we feel threatened. In fact, this is an essential part of what it has kept our species alive for hundreds of thousands of years. But in the modern workplace is not always helpful. We get a lot of false positives because we face increasingly ambiguous situations at work.

Being aware of such false positives, and the frequency with which they happen, is one of the best ways to intercept defensive responses when they are not necessary. By bringing conscious and deliberate attention to situations that we perceive as ambiguous, we can begin to get a better read on the valence of the situation— that is, whether it is negative or positive or neutral. From there, we can engage the neocortex and take appropriate action.

AWARENESS IS THE FIRST STEP

Working with the sympathetic nervous system is not a simple thing. After all, it is part of our autonomic nervous system and runs, for the most part, automatically. There are several things, however, that you can do to manage your sympathetic nervous response and your fight or flight reactions.

The first of these is raising your levels of awareness to your bodily sensations. Whether you are in a stressful situation, a threatening situation, or an enjoyable situation, a deep knowledge and understanding of how your body feels in those situations is powerful information.

Because the amygdala sends information to your body so quickly, your body receives and acknowledges the information before the critical thinking portion of your brain does. The human body is a terrific barometer. When you learn to recognize the information in real time as it shows up in the body, you may gain an edge in regulating your response. You can slow down and deliberately engage your critical thinking skills so that the rational mind and executive function get an opportunity to process the information. That is to say, with a conscious recognition of the information your body is giving you, you may be able to take more deliberate action instead of merely reacting instinctually.

How can you develop the skill to slow this process down and be more in touch with your fight or flight triggers? I recommend two different techniques, detailed below.

The first practical way to develop this skill is to keep a journal of bodily sensations, often referred to as a body journal. At various intervals throughout the day, check in with your body to see what sensations you are feeling. Jot down the time of day, what you were doing, and what you notice in your body.

Begin with a quick scan of your body, top to bottom. Notice if anything feels off or out of whack. You might notice that there is tension in your shoulders or that your neck hurts. (Did you just relax your shoulders after reading that last sentence?) You might realize that you have been clenching your fists or furrowing your brow. You might find that every time you receive an email from a certain colleague your shoulders raise up to your ears and your upper back feels strained. Maybe their name in the "Sender" column is all it takes to generate that reaction. Or you might find interacting with someone else makes you feel relaxed and at ease. Record these reactions in your journal.

In addition to checking in with your body regularly, also check in when something stressful happens. Your sympathetic nervous system, the fight or flight response, will be triggered and your body will be reacting. Notice what you feel and experience at those times and record them in your journal as well.

The more skill you develop in understanding how fight or flight shows up in your body, the more seamlessly you can react to reevaluate when necessary, and the more likely you will be to ensure that what comes out of your mouth is indeed influenced by your *rational* mind. Your faster reaction time will also help tremendously when you need to correct for a false positive, that is, when you perceive a threat that is not actually threatening.

Secondly, meditation and other mindfulness practices can have a measurable impact on how you respond to stress. Meditation can allow you to cope better in difficult situations. The goal of meditation, after all, is to become more mindful and intentional in where you place your focus and how you respond to stimuli in your environment. Indeed, this goal is in line with having a faster response time to false positive "hits" on the sympathetic nervous system. While there is no shortage of information available on meditation, yoga, and other mindfulness practices, it is worth briefly discussing a simple technique that can help you regulate your emotions in times of stress.

A simple place to start is by spending five minutes in meditation two times each day. Even the busiest person has ten minutes to spare. Set a timer for five minutes and silence the voices in your head, the concerns of the day, and any thoughts that may come up. When thoughts do come up, as they inevitably will, thank them and send them on their way. Do not worry about doing it wrong. Meditation has no right or wrong.

As you get comfortable with creating a still mind for five minutes twice a day, begin to lengthen the amount of time you spend in meditation during each session. Grow your practice in very small increments. Move from five minutes at a time to six minutes at a time. Maintain that practice for a week before adding another minute to each session.

Eventually you will develop mastery in producing a quiet mind on demand. Imagine: silence in your brain anytime you want. No critical voices from your past. No worrying. No wondering what other people will think. No replaying past conversations over and over in your mind. Just silence and a still mind. When and where you want it. Priceless.

In keeping a body journal and in developing a meditation practice you will develop speed in gaining control over your reactions and be able to communicate more effectively in high stakes situations and in times of stress. Your fight or flight response will no longer be single-handedly running the show. The executive function of your brain will play a more significant role in how you respond.

CONCLUSION

In this chapter, we've discussed the relationship between the sympathetic nervous system's fight or flight response and your ability to communicate clearly and effectively. When we perceive threat, we are biologically predisposed to respond with defensiveness. If we listen to the cues our body provides when we feel threatened, we can gather more information about what is occurring and in so doing, gain more control.

In the next chapter, we look specifically at stress and its impact on the body and, in turn, communication.

EXERCISES

#1: Your List of Conversations

What are the difficult conversations you have queued up, the ones you have yet to hold? Who are they with and what are they about? Getting that down on paper is the first step toward holding them. It also releases you from some of the angst you have about holding those conversations.

Make a list of the people and topics you have not yet addressed. It's okay if you have more than one topic with the same person. Put them all on the list.

Person	Topic	When

#2: Ghosts of Conversations Past

Many people avoid holding difficult conversations because they remember a time when they had a conversation on a difficult topic that did not go well. When memories of conversations that went poorly continue to haunt you, it will be daunting to try again.

Let's expose the ghosts for what they are: phantoms that belong squarely in the past. Review them one last time, and then let them go so they no longer haunt you.

Make a list of any conversations that you recall that did not go well. Then, remind yourself that that was then and this is now. You are developing a new set of tools to tackle those situations with grace and diplomacy, even if they didn't go well in the past.

Your list:

CHAPTER 2

What's Stress
Got to Do with It?

Unbeknownst to Charlie, a manager in a large financial organization, his direct reports would have a secret meeting every
morning just after he arrived at the office—to discuss nothing
other than Charlie's mood. After a few of them had initial interactions with him first thing in the morning, the team would
gather quickly to discuss Charlie's disposition. Most often he
was irritable and demanding. His staff would rally their support for one another and vow to be available when his inevitable outbursts came. The team knew all too well that, left unchecked, Charlie's bad mood would make for a universally
miserable day for all of them.

Charlie had no idea of how much his emotions were visible
to others. Nor did he understand that they were, in fact,
spreading stress throughout the organization.

Much has been said about stress and its negative impact on the
body and brain. Already in this book, we've explored some of the
negative impacts of stressful situations on communication. Our

goal, however, is not to live a completely stress-free life. Some stress, positive stress, is in fact good for us and helps us get things done and communicate well. When we feel the nudge of positive stress, we are more inclined to meet our deadlines, be productive and bring our best to our work and life.

ZERO TO TERROR IN 60

Neuroscience brings us a framework for considering our level of cognitive arousal and how that impacts our ability to, indeed, bring our best to our work and life. The Arousal Continuum (see Figure 1) shows the progression from a relatively calm state to full-on terror.

Figure 1: Arousal continuum

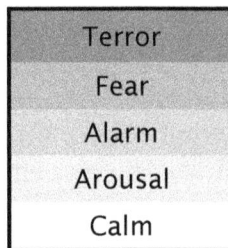

Terror
Fear
Alarm
Arousal
Calm

How does this relate to communication? The relative state of a person's arousal in a conversation has everything to do with how that conversation goes. Different portions of the brain are active in each of the states. As an individual moves up the arousal continuum, he or she has less ability to regulate thoughts and emotions.

When we are calm, the neocortex and cortex regions of the brain are activated and are regulating our thoughts and emotions. This is where we do our best abstract thinking (i.e., strategy, innovation). When we become aroused or interested in something, our cortex and limbic regions of the brain are activated. It is here where we do our best concrete thinking (i.e., planning, creating frameworks from earlier abstract thinking). This state has been described as "relaxed alertness," when one is both relaxed and emotionally engaged simultaneously. It is deemed by educators as a foundational component of being able to learn new skills.[5]

When we become alarmed, the limbic and midbrain regions of the brain are activated and begin regulating our thoughts. We are more likely to react emotionally. As alarm escalates to fear, the midbrain and brainstem, or primitive brain which is responsible for basic survival functions, begin to regulate our reactions. In a state of fear, we are reactive and are less able to be rational. When fear turns to terror, the primitive brain is responsible for regulating behavior. We are completely reflexive and are entirely focused on responding to threat.

The higher we are on the arousal continuum, the less likely we are to control or regulate our emotions or our thoughts. Research in education also explains that the higher on the continuum a learner is, the less capable he or she is of learning new content or retrieving content he or she had mastered in the past (this explains test anxiety, for example).[6]

This helps us understand why it is so hard to think clearly and communicate well in times of duress. It also shows, however, that not all stress is bad. Moving from abstract thinking when the brain is relatively calm to concrete thinking when the brain is in a state of arousal is necessary for moving from concept to action. We may philosophize all day long about a project and not take any action on it if we remain calm and only our neocortex is activated.

When an individual is calm, the stress hormones cortisol and adrenaline are routinely at lower levels, and the whole body, including the brain, functions well. When stress (e.g., a tight deadline at work) is introduced, the body and the brain respond with an elevated state of alertness. This elevated state of alertness assists in greater attention to detail, memory retention, and a heightened sense of urgency.[7] Overall, people may be more creative, collaborative, connected, and innovative as a result of a slight rise in the stress hormones cortisol and adrenaline.

This translates to our communication, as well. Interpersonal communication may be more fluid, rational, and effective. Words may come more readily and precisely. This, for example, is why writers respond well to deadlines. The sense of urgency moves them from an abstract state where the neocortex is working through ideas, to a more concrete state of arousal where the cortex and the limbic systems prompt them to take action. Words are put down on the page. The writer enters a state of focused writing and the first draft gets completed.

Essentially, when things get interesting (read: mildly stressful), the sympathetic nervous system is aroused. If the brain is well-rested, it uses that burst of hormones to create a little extra pressure and rise to the challenge.

STRESS TO BOOST BRAINPOWER

Research supports the idea that some stress is helpful in obtaining better outcomes at work. A study in the Journal of Personality and Social Psychology recently reported that "activating moods" (e.g., happy, elated, fearful, angry) led to more creativity and originality than "deactivating moods" (being sad, depressed, relaxed or serene).[8] The researchers found people's creativity levels went up when they felt positive, and their persistence levels increased when the emotional tone was negative. This is true only up to a point, however. When the valence or tone of the emotional state was too negative (e.g., furious, terrified), the sympathetic nervous system moved into survival mode and the prefrontal cortex shut down.

It is critical for effective communication that we remain along the lower portion of the arousal continuum. When the brain is operating on the high end of the continuum in a state of fear or terror, the ability to regulate thoughts and emotions is significantly reduced and our ability to communicate well is compromised. Rather than sharing careful, well-reasoned responses, we react and shoot off our mouths, becoming both defensive of our own position and offensive, attempting to hurt the other person as a form of protection for ourselves. This is our primitive brain in action.

When we understand that this is the basic hard wiring all humans are issued, it becomes easier to have compassion for a person who may be enraged and flying off the handle. To a certain degree, he or she can't help it. (Of course, the more they practice the exercises outlined in Chapter 1, the more likely it is that they will be able to put some space between stimulus and response.)

This understanding also provides significant motivation to keep from getting too far up the arousal continuum in conversation yourself, knowing that you will not be able to regulate your emotions and thoughts well, the higher you go. If you do move rapidly up the continuum, you may say things you later wish you hadn't. Instead, you want to bring your best contribution to the conversation, including your best critical thinking and your best listening. You cannot do that when you are in a state of fear or terror. Biologically, it is impossible.

Perhaps even more motivating is the notion that in preventing the person you are speaking with from getting to the higher end of the arousal continuum, you are helping them bring their best critical thinking and listening skills to the conversation. That way, they can participate fully. And, when addressing a difficult topic or situation, it is imperative for all parties to bring their best critical thinking skills and listening skills to the table if a well-reasoned conclusion or agreement is to be reached.

Stress at Work

Granted, it is not always easy to remain calm at work. A variety of workplace situations can lead to excessive stress, not to mention stressful situations outside of work that are with us on the job. When I conduct workshops, people tell me the following characteristics are the hallmarks of the most challenging situations and people they deal with:

- Intense emotions
- Defensiveness
- Denial
- Resistance
- Deceit
- Passive-aggressive behavior
- Manipulation
- Blaming
- Bullying
- Condescension
- Aggression
- Righteousness

These are stress-inducing triggers to be sure!

Additionally, when workloads are excessively high for long periods of time, an employee may regularly be operating in a stress-induced state of alarm or fear. Or, if managers or colleagues are disrespectful to their employees or counterparts, those people may experience feelings of fear and the consequent need to defend themselves. Likewise, passive-aggressive behavior may create a sense of alarm or fear for the people who are affected.

If these and other negative behaviors are allowed to continue unchecked, the results are harmful to an organization's culture, to employees' productivity, and ultimately to the bottom line. As the body prepares for fight or flight, the brain may lose its ability to be creative, to collaborate, to connect with others, or to innovate.

On the other hand, when communication is respectful and non-threatening, those same brain receptors easily absorb new information and can process that new information with greater clarity, accuracy, and acumen. When stress levels are typically low to mid-range, the corresponding body and brain states encourage synthesis, new idea generation, and connection with other people. There are significant reasons to keep people in the low to mid-range on the arousal continuum, in terms of both getting the best work out of them and enabling them to communicate most effectively with colleagues and clients alike.

In a relatively calm state, communication is dynamic and fluid and meaning is created almost effortlessly, even when differing opinions are at play. A sense of safety and security is a precursor for remaining in this state. If an individual is concerned that she may lose her job over a simple mistake, for example, she may be so fearful that she doesn't bring her best thinking to her work. Indeed, she will be more likely to make the mistakes that will lead to her firing, thus completing a vicious circle. On the other hand, a sense of security brings with it the ability to more readily address difficult situations and topics, knowing that a free-flowing exchange of ideas may occur, without repercussion or retaliation.

PSYCHOLOGICAL SAFETY

That sense of security can be thought of as psychological safety in the workplace. Essentially, psychological safety means that an individual feels confident enough to take risks among their counterparts. Studies demonstrate positive outcomes for organizations with a high degree of psychological safety amongst their members. Research at the University of Illinois at Urbana-Champaign found that when psychological safety was high, an organization was more likely to adopt process changes and innovations and have them remain sustainable over long periods of time.[9] Additional research indicates that when psychological safety is high, employees can learn better from their mistakes, are more committed and engaged, and are more likely to bring innovative thinking to their work.[10, 11]

A lack of psychological safety makes it harder for individuals to work well with others or exhibit a learning mindset, whereas a strong sense of psychological safety encourages a learning mindset and a willingness to speak up. Research by Dr. Abraham Carmeli and colleagues found that those who felt they had high-quality relationships with their colleagues also felt a higher level of psychological safety and were more likely to have higher levels of learning behavior.[12] That is, there was a correlation between psychological safety and the ability to learn and contribute to a culture of learning within the company.

Additionally, researchers Ingrid Nembhard and Amy Edmondson found that psychological safety was higher for individuals who had higher professional status within their organizations.[13] The researchers suggest that their senior positions create a sense of safety that enables them to speak up in the organization.

Psychological safety is inextricably linked to our communication in the workplace. Being willing to speak up, especially on difficult topics, without fear of retribution or repercussion is of critical importance at work. In a psychologically safe environment, both employees and leaders are empowered to address tough situations head on, without creating feelings of alarm or terror in their colleagues. They'll also be less likely to fear negative consequences for themselves, making them more likely to bring up complicated or challenging issues. Those issues, when solved, will have a positive impact on the organization. Left unspoken, uncomfortable or difficult situations often go from bad to worse. Rarely, if ever, do they resolve themselves.

FROM ABSTRACT TO CONCRETE: PUTTING KNOWLEDGE INTO ACTION

Let's move from abstract thinking (calm, remember?) to concrete thinking (arousal) and discover how to implement the concepts discussed in this chapter. How can you take action on this information? How do you keep your own fear of threats in check? How do you communicate with others such that they retain their ability to regulate their emotions and thinking?

As we discussed in the previous chapter, when you bring your awareness to something you can be more mindful and intentional about your responses to it. To develop increased awareness of how you respond to various stimuli, keep a log of your state of arousal on the continuum. Log events and note how you react to them on the arousal continuum. After you have at least a week's worth of data, analyze the information. What trends are you able to identify? Which are the specific situations or people that cause your response to spike up the continuum, hampering your ability to think critically? Once you have identified any triggers, review the techniques at the end of Chapter 1 to develop additional mastery over your responses to those situations and people.

As important as it is for you to be aware of and regulate your own responses, it doesn't help if the other person responds with fear or terror. To prevent another person's response from hijacking an effective interaction, try to conduct your conversations in a way that will keep their reactions on the lower part of the continuum.

The best thing to ward off fear and terror in the mind of the other person is a strong relationship. When trust and respect are present and the relationship is sound, the other person will be less likely to have a knock-down-drag-out freak out on you. Determine the relative strength of your relationship with those who increase your state of arousal. If the relationship is not strong, set to work on shoring it up. With strong relationships in place, difficult situations are easier to handle.

CONCLUSION

In this chapter, we reviewed the effect stress has on our ability to communicate clearly and effectively. Although stress often gets a bad reputation, it is not without practical utility. Low to moderate amounts of stress heighten our awareness and bring our surroundings into crisp focus. We can connect, collaborate, and communicate easily with others. On the other hand, when we experience extreme stress, we no longer feel psychologically safe, our brain does not easily take in new information, and our ability to communicate effectively is hampered.

In the next chapter, we will look more closely at the brain, including four distinct regions of the brain and their operation's effect on optimal communication.

EXERCISES

#3: Your Inner Compass

We all have an inner compass that points us toward safety and away from danger. This week, listen closely to your inner compass. Who are the people and what are the activities that made you feel the most comfortable and safe? Who are the people and what are the activities that, this week, felt dangerous?

Comfortable and safe:

Dangerous:

#4: Arousal Log

Using the Arousal Continuum, for the next two weeks, log events that trigger alarm, fear, or terror. Recall that the higher you are on the continuum, the less regulation you have over your thoughts and emotions. Identifying situations in which it seemed like you had little emotional or thought regulation is a good place to start.

Log the stimuli that prompted your arousal (what happened) as well as when the situation occurred and which state on the continuum you reached (alarm, fear or terror).

Once you have two weeks of data, analyze your experiences for trends. Are there certain people or situations that are triggers? Which tools from this chapter will best help you control your emotional response?

What happened	Who	When	Arousal state

CHAPTER 3

Inside the Brain: A Choreography of Stimulus and Response

"All ready for the board presentation tomorrow, Jason?" Heather asked as she joined her colleague waiting for the elevator.

"What do you mean?" retorted Jason, a little more quickly and more harshly than he'd intended.

Unbeknownst to her, Heather had struck a nerve with Jason. He'd been asked to present to the board of directors 18 months earlier and it did *not* go well. In fact, Jason had received harsh criticism about it from multiple people. Now, a year and a half later, he was invited back to present again. A chance at redemption is how he saw it.

Jason's sharp response to Heather, whose intent was merely to make small talk while they waited for the elevator, was governed by a primitive part of his brain designed to sense threats and provide protection. Accordingly, he reacted to Heather's off-handed question as it were a threat to his self-concept rather than small talk. While Heather hadn't meant to make him question his worth or his identity, he reacted from the part of his brain that was responsible for exactly that.

This chapter explains four evolutionarily distinct regions of the brain and how they react and interact when confronted with threatening or potentially threatening situations and consequently affect communication. As you will see, when these distinct "brains" are functioning in harmony, a careful and complex choreography allows us to express our best ideas, be of social and emotional support to others, reason and solve problems, create and innovate, and discuss challenging situations effectively.

Each of the four regions plays a vital role in understanding threatening and potentially threatening situations and how we respond to them. From sensing stimuli to having an emotional reaction to using critical thinking skills and making decisions that require abstract thinking, all the regions of the brain are important and play a significant role in how we hold difficult conversations.

THE RESPONSIVE BRAIN

The first three of these four regions were initially proposed as the *triune* brain, or three-part brain, by Dr. Paul MacLean in the 1950s and 1960s.[14] He proposed that as the human brain evolved over time, it "upgraded" itself to include functions that handled increasingly complex thought processes. MacLean hypothesized that these regions of the brain developed in bursts in our evolution. While that part of his theory remains in question, his description of the brain's organization has endured the test of time. The triune brain structure is organized hierarchically, with survival instincts on the bottom and more abstract thinking on top. While contemporary experts in neuroscience may find this an oversimplified explanation of how the various parts of the brain work together, for our purposes, the regions MacLean identified hold value and shine a light on what is occurring before, during and after a difficult conversation.

R-Brain

Brian cringed every time his manager, Russ, stopped by his desk. Russ was a perfectionist and was easily angered when things weren't perfect. Brian seemed to bear the brunt of his anger more than others on the team. It seemed to Brian that every time Russ stopped by, his purpose was to tell Brian about that latest round of things he'd done wrong. Consequently, Brian was self-conscious and worried much of the time, which resulted in more errors in his work. It also resulted in him shutting down when Russ came near.

Brian's R-brain was running the show. The most primitive and first brain—in evolutionary terms—is what Dr. MacLean referred to as the reptilian brain or R-brain. The R-brain has much in common with the brains of modern-day reptiles (hence the name) and it regulates most autonomic functions like breathing, heart rate, and body temperature. This region of the brain is completely instinctual and focused on survival. It includes the amygdala, which we discussed in Chapter 1. MacLean proposed that this region of the brain is instrumental to human survival. Instinctual behaviors such as aggression, dominance, and territoriality originate in the R-brain and serve to ward off threats and provide safety. Some neuroscientists affectionately refer to the activities this part of the brain handles as the Four Fs: feeding, fighting, fleeing, and fornicating.

In a difficult conversation, this is the part of the brain that assesses whether a threat is present. Thus, the R-brain's job is to promote safety. Given that responsibility, the fight or flight response is invoked when threat is sensed, as described in Chapter 2. Brian's brain assessed a threat every time Russ came near and his fear triggered a fight or flight response that caused him to run away or shut down.

M-Brain

Latoya, a vice president at a major information technology company, reflected on the most recent round of interviews she'd conducted for a managerial position that reported to her. The strongest candidate by far was someone who didn't fit the typical career path leading to the role. Instead of a corporate background, this candidate was a professor. Latoya paused, wondering why this candidate was the best choice. While the pedigree of the candidate didn't fit the corporate expectations, Latoya's intuition kicked in and she *knew* that this was the right candidate, without a doubt.

Latoya's M-brain was dominant in her assessment. The second brain is the mammalian brain, or M-brain. It is the region of the brain that houses the limbic system. It is the brain of instinct and emotion. It records memories and powerful experiences, whether positive or negative. It houses the regions of the brain that are responsible for learning and memory as well. The M-brain is at the heart of the value judgments we make, often unconsciously, and influences our behavior tremendously. This portion of the brain also provides flexibility in behavior so that we are able to adapt to changing circumstances. Finally, this portion of the brain integrates messages from both inside and outside the body and is thus central to our sense of personal identity.

As it relates to communication in general and difficult conversations in particular, the M-brain plays a very important role. Emotional bonding between people, whether it is parent-to-child or coworker-to-coworker, originates from this part of the brain. This is what Latoya felt as she interviewed the professor for the management position: an emotional bond, the flexibility to hire a non-traditional candidate, and a connection between how the decision felt in her head and her body.

When one person feels the emotional bond and another doesn't, or when one person is able to demonstrate flexible behavior and another isn't, conditions are ripe for a difficult conversation. Another way that the M-Brain is can create conditions for a difficult conversation is when there is a threat to personal identity. It may happen, as in the opening story with Heather and Jason, that one person's seemingly innocuous comment opens a disparity in another person's self-concept or personal identity. That leads to defensiveness and the context for a difficult conversation is set.

Neocortex

Kristen had a difficult choice ahead of her. An employee she'd hired 12 months ago, Sarah, wasn't quite measuring up to expectations. On paper and in the interview process, the new employee looked great. But a year into the role, Sarah was meeting only minimum expectations when performing her job duties. Kristen had addressed this as the 90-day probationary period came to an end, again in one-on-one meetings, and most recently at her first annual performance evaluation. Now Kristen was faced with the tough decision whether to let Sarah go or double down on coaching her to perform at and above the expected levels. Kristen took out a piece of paper and began to make a pro/con list.

Kristen was using her third brain. The third brain is the neo-mammalian brain. It consists primarily of the neocortex, which is the center of higher-order thinking, sometimes referred to as the executive function of the brain. The neocortex interprets complex stimuli such as sights and sounds into coherent messages. This portion of the brain is primarily concerned with what is happening in the external world and keeping us safe. For example, it is more concerned with accurately judging if it is safe to cross the street at a busy intersection than it is with what temperature it is. (Although, if it were 20 below zero and we weren't dressed for the weather, this part of our brain may be more concerned with finding warmth than crossing the street safely.)

It is in this region of the brain that reasoning, logic, and learning take place. This is where our day-to-day decision making occurs: what to wear, whom to hire, how many hours to allocate for work on a project, or whether to apply for a promotion. It is also where what we commonly think of as the activities of "consciousness" occur: introspection, self-awareness, planning, and language. This part of the brain worries, gets self-conscious, and carefully considers word choices when communicating.

Clearly, this part of the brain is of critical importance as it relates to decision making and communication on difficult topics. As Kristen prepared to talk with Sarah about next steps, she knew she had to bring her best critical thinking and analysis to both the preparation and the conversation itself. Anything less than optimal performance from this part of the brain would lead to suboptimal results. When we are tired, sick, or engaged in a fight or flight response, this portion of the brain is not fully functioning, and during a full-on fight or flight response, the neocortex can essentially go offline. When the neocortex is offline, language, abstract thought, imagination, and curiosity become all but inoperable. These are just the skills we need when facing a difficult interpersonal situation.

Prefrontal Cortex

Maria was irritated with her colleague, Sanjay. Sanjay's habit of interrupting her during meetings was bothering her almost to the point of her not being able to participate. She hesitated to bring her best ideas to the table only to have Sanjay cut her off in mid-sentence. Maria worked with me as her coach to help her get some emotional distance so she could respond assertively in those situations, without withdrawing (usually seething at Sanjay in her head). She also wanted to be able to respond without becoming overly aggressive and unprofessional with an outburst fueled by anger. I shared with her some techniques for controlling her emotional response to the situation (you'll find them in the next chapter) so that she could identify the situation, the consequent reaction, and accompanying thought pattern that emerged, and then finally, actively choose how she wanted to respond.

Maria was working on developing the power of her fourth brain. The prefrontal cortex, or the fourth brain, located in the front of the brain, inside the neocortex, is associated with the more abstract and uniquely human practices such as creative thinking, making music, and inventing things. The prefrontal cortex is engaged when we exercise creativity, innovation, and imagination. It is also the part of the brain that is involved in the expression of personality, complex decision making, and moderating social behavior. This is where we grapple with conflicting thoughts, evaluate choices, predict outcomes, work toward complex goals, and explore the potential consequences of our actions.

The prefrontal cortex is particularly important at work. Innovation, creativity, complex problem solving, controlling emotional responses, and communicating with sensitivity are all critical in today's workplace. These were the areas where Maria was working toward gaining more mastery. As she knew, being able to communicate ideas, express creativity, and reason with others when solving complex problems all require astute communication skills.

When our four "brains" function in harmony in the workplace—that is, when our R-brain is dutifully keeping us alive while our M-brain is accurately distinguishing threats from opportunities, our neocortex is applying reason and logic, and our prefrontal cortex is allowing ideas to comingle and creating new connections—then, and only then, are we able to communicate optimally at work. Recall the arousal continuum discussed in the previous chapter. When the brain is aroused moderately, it is at its most alert and high functioning level. We can express our best ideas, learn and retain new information, be of social and emotional support to others, reason and solve problems, create and innovate, and discern which of all the available responses is most appropriate in a given situation. Accordingly, what comes out of the mouth is more fully informed by the brain (or, in another sense, all four "brains").

When a person suddenly explodes in an emotional outburst, it is the R-brain in the lead. Meanwhile, the more advanced thinking of the neocortex is hindered during this outburst. The person may be fully conscious of the behavior but incapable of immediately changing the behavior or bringing it under control. Oftentimes, people report that they feel like two different individuals in such circumstances: the one who is doing the acting, or having the emotional outburst (R-brain and M-brain), and the one who is observing the behavior (neocortex).

In sum, each of these regions of the brain is responsible for differing functions, all of which contribute to communicating optimally. The regions allow for more abstract thinking over time, moving from simple to complex. The R-brain's responsibility is in the realm of survival. The M-brain distinguishes threats and alerts you to them. The neocortex reasons and applies logic. The prefrontal cortex connects ideas and enables creativity.

Figure 2: Communication responses and the parts of the brain

Triune Brain			
R-Brain	M-Brain	Neocortex	Prefrontal Cortex
Reptilian	Mammalian	Rational	Combining
Instinctive	Intuitive	Calm, slow, steady	Deliberate
Safety	Values, feelings	Focus	Creativity
Autonomic	Limbic	Abstract	Associative
Simple ⟶			*Complex*

STIMULUS-RESPONSE

Nicole was embarrassed and frustrated. Whenever she was in the presence of senior leaders and she was asked a question (which was frequent, since she was their finance liaison), she would grow nervous and stammer. She thought back to the first time it had happened. It was after she'd taken a lateral transfer from another division. Her title and role remained the same, and she mistakenly thought expectations would be the same as well. When she attended her first meeting with the new senior leadership team, she'd come unprepared. No one briefed her that she would be asked questions or was expected to participate. She was asked budgetary questions that she was unprepared to answer and she stumbled and stammered rather than answering cogently.

Her stammering at the first meeting was something she couldn't seem to shake. Nicole had developed a stimulus-response pattern in which the stimulus was being asked a question in a meeting by a senior leader and her automatic response was to get nervous and stammer—even when she knew the answer! As we discussed in Chapter 1, the stimulus-response cycle is difficult to break. The more intense the threat, the more likely we will be to respond instinctually and with intensity.

In the short term, when you experience a threat, you can train yourself to manage it more productively. The R-brain and the M-brain are responding to the threat instinctually and there is no stopping the stimulus from triggering the brain. The perceived threat may be a false positive, meaning your brain is making a mistake in interpreting an event as a threat. For Nicole even in later meetings when she was prepared, a two-fold response pattern was still triggered automatically. The first response manifested in her body (think rapid heartbeat, sweaty palms, etc.). The second part was the reaction she had in response to the stimulus. Here is where there is an opportunity to put some space between stimulus and response. One of the exercises at the end of this chapter will assist with that. It will not entirely break the stimulus-response cycle, but with conscious effort you can learn to manage it better. Next, we turn our attention to undesirable stimulus-response patterns that repeat themselves.

UNWANTED REPETITIVE PATTERNS

Brandon and Kate were at it again.

Another staff meeting where Kate and Brandon were on the opposite sides of the same coin: Kate, advocating for an engineering schedule that was realistic and didn't compromise the health or safety of her crew and Brandon, fiercely arguing for a faster delivery to their clients. This pattern was a near weekly occurrence in the project management meeting.

Morgan, the project manager, had spoken to each of them privately just before the meeting. They each shared a genuine desire to be more amicable and see the situation from the other person's point of view before reacting. But publicly in the meeting, their behavior was nowhere near amicable. It was the same pattern repeating itself again and again. Their pattern was not one of sharing respectful differences. Rather, their behavior was unprofessional and ego bruising, their words like daggers.

Frustrated, Morgan spoke to each of them privately again after the meeting. She had to get to the bottom of this disagreement before it put the project in jeopardy. How could they have earnestly promised to comport themselves more professionally and then act like small children throwing sand during the meeting?

Brandon and Kate were caught in an unwanted repetitive pattern (URP), a sequential and recurring episode of conflict that is considered unwanted by those in the conflict (not to mention those around them!). This phenomenon was first named by researchers at the University of Massachusetts who were curious about why a particular pair of other faculty members routinely became polarized on the professional topics they discussed in the course of their job duties. Although both colleagues who sparred wanted to be amicable and professional, they quickly escalated "into extended, hostile and ego-scarring duels."[15]

URPs are a classic combination of the R-brain and the M-brain sensing a threat and the neocortex and the prefrontal cortex responding efficiently, executing the response it has habitually enacted in similar situations in the past. For many who begin to recognize their URPs, they often feel like two separate people, as discussed earlier in this chapter: the R-brain and M-Brain doing the acting and the neocortex watching the scene unfold.

URPs develop because two people have fallen into a pattern or script that demands each of them behave in a conflicting manner. Often, the pattern one person follows serves to fuel the negativity of the other and that person responds negatively in turn. Then, rinse and repeat.

Brandon and Kate each told Morgan essentially the same thing in their private meetings: "I couldn't help it, I had no choice but to stick up for [the customer/the engineering team]."

Brandon and Kate will continue to enact their URP until the unwritten scripts they are following get interrupted. Either one of them could deliberately choose to behave differently of their own accord or Morgan, the project manager, could choose to structure the meeting and the conversation in a way that won't let the URP get a chance to take hold.

When a URP is detected, it is important to understand first, that the person or persons involved feel like they have no choice. Their experience in the moment is that there is no possible alternate response. The second aspect that is important to understand is that there indeed is another choice. In fact, there are myriad ways in which to respond. It requires deliberate action to think of one of those other ways to respond and to enact it. Exercise Six at the end of this chapter will assist with breaking URPs.

We know we can't easily control the R-brain. We know that when it perceives a threat, it creates a reaction in our bodies. We can listen closer to the response of our M-brain and tap into our intuition and flexibility. And we can build in a space between stimulus and response so that what comes out of our mouth (or keyboard!) is influenced as much by the prefrontal cortex and the neocortex as it is the R-Brain and the M-brain.

CONCLUSION

The four evolutionarily distinct regions of the brain are responsible for different functions. When the R-brain, M-brain, neocortex, and prefrontal cortex are working together, we are not only able to respond in the manner most appropriate to the situation, we are also able to bring our best thinking to the interaction.

In the next section, you will learn a step-by-step process for facilitating a difficult conversation in a manner that keeps defensiveness at bay, in you and also in the other person.

EXERCISES

#5: Retrospective Analysis

Unfortunately, it isn't likely that we will "catch" our brain in the act of performing a communication pattern that doesn't positively serve our workplace relationships. In fact, it is far more likely that the R-brain and the M-brain's intent activity on survival will preclude us from stopping nearly any intense reaction to a threat as it happens. However, later when the adrenaline, cortisol, norephedrine, and other stress hormones have subsided, it is possible to do a retrospective analysis of a communication situation gone bad.

Follow the steps below to conduct a retrospective analysis on communication gone awry and determine what you can do differently next time you are in a similar situation.

1. What happened? List the facts, being as objective as possible.
2. What was your reaction? Specifically, how did you behave, what did you say or do?
3. What triggered you to have a defensive (or otherwise undesirable) response?
4. What physical response did you have (pounding heart, clenched fists, etc.)?
5. What response would you have rather taken?
6. Use your response from question #4 to catch yourself and slow down next time so that you can put some distance between your stimulus and response and choose the response you listed in question #5.

#6: Breaking Unwanted Repetitive Patterns

If you have identified a URP that you would like to discontinue, you will need to examine the belief that you are obligated to react in a certain way. If you find yourself thinking, "I had no choice. I had to react that way," you have mostly likely identified a URP. Follow the steps below to break the rules that govern the URP so that you can get a different outcome.

1. Who is the other party in this URP?

2. Under what circumstances or conditions does this URP present itself?

3. What would you like to have happen instead of the URP?

4. What do you need to say or do differently in order for that to happen?

5. Try that new behavior the next time you are in a similar situation with the person who triggers the URP.

6. Record your reactions. What specifically did you say or do differently? What was the other person's reaction? Were you able to break the URP? What will you do in the next similar situation?

Part 2

Difficult Conversations: Step by Step

CHAPTER 4

Preparing for the Conversation

"Some days you can't win for losing," I thought as I parked my car and headed into the office. It was a rough morning and it wasn't even eight o'clock yet.

I was in a corporate job, and in those days it wasn't uncommon for me to have a morning that went something like this, and in fact, I once had a morning that went exactly like this: I woke up, showered and ate breakfast, got the kids ready for school, argued briefly with my husband over something inconsequential, and left for work with two kids in tow. I dropped my daughter off at preschool, only to discover that we'd left her spare change of clean clothes at home (she'd worn them the previous day and her regular clothes had come home "soiled"). I then dropped my middle-schooler off at his school just as he realized his homework folder was on the breakfast table at home.

"I am *not* a helicopter parent," I repeated to myself as I went back to the house, collected the forgotten items and delivered them to their respective schools. I stopped briefly to refill my gas tank and just as I came up to speed on the highway, in my rearview mirror I saw my gas cap bounce across the pavement and land in the ditch. Ughh.

I arrived at the office and my first order of business was to have a conversation with one of my direct reports about his working style (gregarious and outgoing, collaborative to an extreme) and how disruptive it was to those on the team who needed a quieter working environment to be able to concentrate and get their work completed on time. Needless to say, my head was not in a space to hold a productive conversation on a potentially difficult topic!

We are not always in the best frame of mind to have a difficult conversation with someone when the need arises. Sometimes we are emotionally distracted or upset and it has nothing to do with the person we need to speak to. Other times we are emotionally distracted or upset and it has *everything* to do with the person we need to talk to.

This chapter is about emotional readiness. It includes an explanation of the value of creating an emotional clearing for the conversation. It also includes techniques for creating that clearing as well as techniques for managing defensive feelings that may emerge within yourself.

Why is this important? Foremost, it would not be fair to my employee if I brought all the frustration and angst from my early morning hours into the conversation with him. Any agitation or distraction that I harbored from those earlier moments have no place in that conversation and would serve as a distraction. In times like these, it is easy to enter into a conversation while you are still in a frustrated, angry, and anxious emotional state that has nothing to do with the person you are talking to.

In other cases, you might be frustrated, angry, and anxious and it has *everything* to do with the person you are about to talk with. If this were the sixth, seventh, or eighth time I'd had this discussion about respecting the working styles of others with my employee, rather than the first or second, I quite likely would be experiencing angst and agitation toward *him* because of our past failure to resolve the issue.

In either case, a distracted emotional state has a bearing on the conversation. When you are experiencing angst and distress and you bring it along to a conversation, especially a challenging one, you are not creating an open and empty "container" in which to have that conversation. You are doing a disservice to both the conversation and the other person.

When you start with a messy head space, you may still get the work of the conversation done, but it will take considerably more time than if you began from a clear head space. I liken it to an artist painting a picture on a canvas. If the artist were given a canvas that already had a picture on it, and you asked her to paint a different picture on top of it, could she do it? Yes, she most likely could. It would take significantly more paint, time, and effort, however, than if you'd given her a blank canvas. Likewise, when we come to a conversation as a blank canvas, we can accomplish that which we set out to do more efficiently and more effectively.

When you enter into a conversation (on a difficult subject or otherwise) in an emotionally clear place, you are no longer tied to the outcomes of the past and you create new possibility in that conversation. Possibility for a new outcome. Possibility for new understanding. Possibility to deepen the relationship. Possibility to hear the other person's side of the story and have them hear yours. Possibility to resolve the situation and reach agreement.

On the other hand, if you are distracted emotionally, you will have a harder time connecting with the other person. If your emotional distraction is caused by a difficult topic of discussion or a challenging relationship with the other person, you are most likely to get a similar result to what you got in the past: a difficult conversation and no resolution.

If your emotional distraction has nothing to do with the other person, you are still doomed to suboptimal results. At best, you will not be fully present with the other person and at worst they will interpret your anger, angst, or anxiety as directed toward them. The solution in either case is to prepare for the conversation by clearing your emotions.

CLEAR YOUR EMOTIONS

The standard practice to prepare for a difficult conversation is to think about what you are going to say and clarify your overall goal for the talk. While this is indeed necessary, it is not sufficient to create the ideal conditions for reliable resolution, understanding, and agreement. Adding the step of clearing your emotions creates a set of conditions that enable you to speak about the challenging topic, address your aims and goals, and do so without distraction. It can also help you create a meaningful connection with the other person. This ups your odds of achieving a deep focus on the issue and fully resolving it so you won't have to revisit it in the future. It also serves to strengthen the relationship.

Imagine that you were going to set up camp in the midst of a dense woods. You would need to clear away brush, dry grasses, and perhaps even trees to create a space in which to camp. Emotional clearing is similar in that it creates a clear, open space, emotionally speaking, in which to have your conversation.

Clearing your emotions enables you to come to the conversation centered on the other person and the topic at hand and to exclude all unrelated matters. Unencumbered by emotional distractions—whether or not they relate your conversational partner—you can be fully present with the person and the situation.

Next we will discuss techniques for creating an emotional clearing and techniques for remaining in that clearing should you begin to feel defensive.

CLEARING TECHNIQUES

There are myriad ways to clear your emotions and create a clear head space. Of the ones discussed here, one or two of them may resonate for you. Or they may prompt you to think of techniques that may be an even better fit for you.

Phone-A-Friend

The first technique is what I call "Phone-A-Friend." It operates something like the Phone-A-Friend "lifeline" did on the show "Who Wants to Be a Millionaire," but with one distinct difference. In the show, the contestant could make a 30 second call to a friend when they were stumped, hoping their friend knew the answer to the question. This Phone-A-Friend technique differs in one important regard: your friend's job is NOT to give you the answer or help solve the problem. Instead, their role is first to listen attentively and really "get" what is bothering you and then to "hold" that problem, issue, or set of experiences while you have the difficult conversation with someone.

Recall the example I shared regarding a rough morning before going into the office where my first order of business was to have a sensitive conversation with one of my staff. I used Phone-A-Friend that morning. When I parked my car at the office and before I went into the building, I called my friend Pam. In that brief phone call, I shared all of the stressful, frustrating, and infuriating things that had happened that morning (it was still before 8:00 AM!). Furthermore, I shared that my first order of business for the workday was to have a conversation on a difficult topic with one of my employees. I told her I wanted to be free from the earlier part of the morning before speaking with my employee.

I shared this all into Pam's voicemail. Then I went into the office and had the difficult conversation. Four hours later, I received a text from Pam that simply said, "Got it." Pam and I have a long history of using the Phone-A-Friend technique to create an emotional clearing for one another. She and I have been on both sides of many similar conversations, creating a clearing for one another when the need arises. As a consequence, her listening in the future is so powerful it helps me in the present (she listened to the voicemail after I'd held the conversation)!

In choosing a Phone-A-Friend partner, there are several tips to keep in mind. First, it should be someone you trust. You don't want this person gossiping to others about the frustrations you entrusted to them. Second, it must be someone who does not have a strong desire to fix things in your life. For most of us that rules out a spouse or partner. Spouses and partners, generally speaking, don't like to see you in distress and they want to fix and solve things for you. A Phone-A-Friend conversation is NOT about fixing and solving anything. It's about listening and just "getting it." Accordingly, your Phone-A-Friend partner must be able to embrace a bit of emotional distance or at least refrain from trying to solve your problems.

Note: It's okay to tell someone how you want them to listen. Before you get into the substance of what you want to share with them, you can say something like this: "I want to tell you about something that's bugging me—don't worry, it's not about you—

before I call my client/mom/ex. I just need you to listen. There's nothing to fix or solve. I just need to be heard by someone before I make that call. Does that make sense?"

Phone-A-Friend is great for verbal processors, those who like to talk things through out loud. We're not all like that, however. The next technique works well for those who are not verbal processors.

Move Your Body

A second clearing technique is exercise or movement. For some, there is nothing like getting physically active and moving their bodies during a favorite sport or activity to help them put their troubles aside. (For others, this may be an anxiety-provoking suggestion that makes them sink deeper into the couch cushions and pull a blanket over their head.) If you do like to hit the gym, select an exercise class, a weight lifting session, or a running or cycling route that will get your blood pumping moderately.

The goal with exercise as a clearing technique is to oxygenate your blood and dissipate the stress hormones (adrenaline, cortisol, norepinephrine) that are coursing through your system. This will assist in creating some emotional distance between you and whatever has a grip on you before you hold that conversation. Aim for low impact exercise, like walking, especially if you are not very physically fit. If you are physically fit, a light jog will work just fine, but keep the intensity low. High intensity exercise is known to increase cortisol levels. The effects of low impact exercise will last several hours so if the conversation is in the morning, get your exercise before you go into the office. If it is in the afternoon, use your lunch break to get that workout in. Be sure to shower or otherwise freshen up before your conversation, otherwise you might find yourself on the receiving end of a difficult conversation about bodily hygiene.

Tidying Up

A third technique is to put something in order. This might mean cleaning the garage or straightening your desk. A key characteristic of this technique is that there must be disorder in that which you are putting order to. For example, if your desk is already reasonably tidy, putting things at right angles is not sufficient to feel like you've made much of a difference. If you are a neat-nik already and this technique appeals to you, you might need to clean someone else's garage or straighten someone else's desk (make sure you ask first!).

When we bring order to chaos, it calms the mind and, like exercise, may allow us to put some emotional distance between ourselves and the situation. And for some people, cleaning the garage, our desk, or our childhood bedroom feels more terrifying than actually having the conversation. If that's the case for you, select another technique.

STAYING CALM

If you've done your preparation, it will be easier to remain calm throughout a conversation on a difficult topic (or if you can't remain calm, at least keep from saying things you might later regret). Speaking of staying calm, telling someone to "calm down" is one of the easiest ways to send them right up the arousal continuum. On the other hand, when you are able to manage your own emotions and remain calm, it helps the other person to do the same.

Human communication is highly reciprocal. Whether we say "Good morning" to someone while walking the dog or smile at a stranger in the grocery store, it is extremely likely that they will do the same in return. In difficult or challenging situations, it is even more important to remember this phenomenon. Perhaps you've been in a grocery store and seen a small child ask for a toy/sugary cereal/candy. "I want that!" It may start innocently enough, and if the child is persistent and not getting the answer she wants, things might escalate. As the child's request turns to a demand, left unchecked, the parent will likely reciprocate the intensity of the child's demand with something along the lines of "No! That will rot your teeth!" This will prompt the child to repeat her demand with greater intensity. It's as if the two are in a poker game and with each go round, they are matching each other and raising the stakes.

This phenomenon occurs in conversations with grown-ups at work just as it does with kids and parents at the grocery store. The phenomenon is called emotional contagion and research demonstrates that we are likely to "catch" the emotional state of someone else. Research by Dr. Sigal Barsade at Yale University, one of the leading experts on emotional contagion, found that not only does the mood of an employee affect other employees, it can also unknowingly have a significant influence on their judgement and on business decisions.[16] Our mood in a difficult situation may be that of anger, frustration, or exasperation (especially if this is the seventeenth time we are addressing this issue with the person!). If we bring frustration or anger into the conversation, the other person is likely to "catch" that mood and the conversation may negatively spiral out of control.

If you're talking with a colleague about his regular habit of clipping his toenails at his desk, which disgusts you, and you enter into that conversation with disgust as your prevalent emotion, there is a good chance your counterpart will become disgusted with you, too. This is not a good place from which to start a conversation on a difficult topic, and things are bound to escalate. I see your disgust and raise you to anger.

Instead, if you can remain calm, there is a far better chance that you and your colleague can reach a new understanding about toenail clipping at the office (let's hope you don't work in a restaurant!). Our general tendency is to match, if not escalate, the emotional intensity of the other. Whether it is in a face-to-face conversation or an email or text exchange, we will tend to match and/or raise the other person's emotional intensity if we are not intentional with our response.

It might happen like this: You receive an email from a colleague who is upset and blaming you for something that recently went wrong. You notice that your boss is copied on the email, as are several other highly respected colleagues. You are infuriated. In a flash, you hit Reply All and add your colleague's boss and several other senior managers. You begin to fire off your response, equal parts defending your own behavior and blaming them for their part. Calm? Hardly.

Calm is easier said than done—especially when the stakes are high or when you or your counterpart are apt to respond with emotional intensity.

Recall the arousal continuum discussed in Chapter 2. Remaining on the calm end of the continuum will bode well for your conversation. Keep in mind that the goal is not to become an emotionless automaton, void of any emotional response whatsoever. When you are sharing with your supervisor the need for a more manageable workload (or your need to be transferred to another part of the building because of your colleague's incessant toenail clipping), it would be inconsistent and perhaps unnerving if you were completely calm and emotionless. Rather, the goal is to keep your emotions in check (rather than erasing them or ignoring them) when starting the conversation and continue to regulate your emotions throughout the conversation.

Keeping emotional contagion in mind, you'll want to regulate your own emotions. If you can keep yourself from escalating up the continuum to fear or terror, you're likely to prevent your counterpart from escalating to that point, as well.

And, as you'll recall from Chapter 2, not only do we lose our ability to regulate our emotions as we move up the continuum, we also lose our ability to regulate our thoughts and think critically. We'll talk more about this in the next chapter, but for now, keep in mind that the emotional state you bring to the conversation has everything to do with how the other person is likely to respond.

Additional Strategies

The strategies we've discussed earlier in this chapter for clearing your emotions will assist in getting calm before a difficult conversation, a critical step in setting the tone of the conversation. Here are several additional strategies for remaining calm during the conversation, whether you initiated the conversation or if the difficult conversation found you and perhaps caught you unawares.

One important strategy is to pay attention to your breath. When you remember to breathe deeply you will help to calm yourself down by getting oxygen to the brain, helping to dissipate the stress hormones cortisol, adrenaline, and norepinephrine. This will allow you to wrangle back access to and control of the executive function of your brain.

Another technique is to connect with a physical object as a reminder to remain on the lower end of the arousal continuum, a method referred to as "anchoring." To anchor, select an object you regularly wear: glasses, a wedding band, a watch, or some other item you are likely to have on your person during challenging situations. When you start to feel your mood escalating, center yourself by touching the object. Use it as an anchor or reminder to manage your emotions and remain calm. While you will know that the simple gesture of placing your hand on your watch is a strategic tool to maintain emotional control, others will not notice the maneuver. The key to using an anchor is to practice connecting with it in at regular intervals, ideally when you are not in a situation that provokes you, but rather when you are simply thinking about how you would respond in a stressful situation. Just as an athlete performs drills or a pilot engages in simulations, so too will your practice set you up for success when a high stakes situation comes along. Your practice sessions will have made a habit of anchoring to your object of choice and you will connect with it readily and use it to center your emotions and act intentionally.

A final technique is to maintain perspective on the situation. If you realize that the situation in the grocery store with your child and the sugary cereal is really not the end of the world as we know it and that children are hard-wired to be persistent, you just may find some grace in the situation, both for yourself and the child. In that moment of grace, you may find an alternate way to persuade them to let go (perhaps literally) of the sugary cereal. "Let's go home and make your favorite muffins for tomorrow's breakfast." Or with your colleague's toenails: while it disgusts you, it isn't likely to take the company down financially. When we get a handle on the relative magnitude of the situation and place it in perspective, we might even laugh. That might not be appropriate given the situation, so laugh quietly.

CONCLUSION

We've looked at techniques for emotional clearing, including Phone-A-Friend, exercise, and organizing. We've also considered strategies for keeping your cool and making sure the conversation stays on track and at the appropriate stress level. Use the following exercises to help you expand your toolkit for emotional readiness as you prepare for difficult conversations.

EXERCISES

#7: Phone-A-Friend

Rather than bring your emotional distractions into a conversation on a challenging topic, drop them off with a friend so you can be free from them. When you Phone-A-Friend, your friend's job is NOT to give you the answer or help solve the problem. Instead, their role is first to listen attentively and really "get" what is bothering you and then to "hold" that problem, issue or set of experiences while you have the difficult conversation with someone.

In choosing a Phone-A-Friend partner, there are several tips to keep in mind.

1. Select someone you trust.
2. It must be someone who does not have a strong desire to fix things in your life.
3. It must be someone who can take your direction on how to listen.

List several people you can "audition" to be your Phone-A-Friend:

#8: Emotional Contagion: Inflaters and Deflaters

Research shows that we are likely to "catch" the emotional state of someone else. Research by Dr. Sigal Barsade at Yale University, one of the leading experts on emotional contagion, found that not only does the mood of individuals affect other employees, it also unknowingly, can have a significant influence on their judgement and on business decisions.

Positive people can infuse you with upbeat emotions. I call them "inflaters" because you can catch their good vibes and that can fill you up with optimism and confidence.

Who are the people in your life who are emotionally contagious and consistently spread positive emotions?

We are just as likely (and sometimes more likely) to "catch" the negative emotional state of someone else. Negative people infect others with their bad attitudes. I call these people "deflaters" because they have a tendency to deflate a good mood if we don't prepare ourselves before connecting with them.

Who are the deflaters—those who are emotionally contagious and consistently spread negative emotions—in your life?

CHAPTER 5

Open Without Defensiveness

Amy was a new member at the YMCA, and she and her family made their first visit there on a recent Saturday morning. After Amy's workout, she collected her children from the Kids Zone and went to the locker room to take a quick shower. Her children, ages four and six, played nearby, rolling an exercise ball back and forth. Unbeknownst to Amy, children under the age of 18 were not permitted in the women's locker room. As Amy's children played quietly and Amy toweled off and dressed, another woman angrily glared in turn at the children and their mother. A patron who took very seriously the "no children" rule, she looked ready to pounce.

Amy had just finished dressing and the observer was about to swoop in to school Amy on the locker room rules. Sensing that trouble was brewing, another woman stepped in and addressed Amy.

"Hi, I'm Michelle. Didn't I just see you in the yoga class?"

"Hi, I'm Amy. Nice to meet you. Yeah, I was in that class. My legs still feel a little wobbly from holding those poses so long!"

"I know what you mean. I'm a regular in Beth's yoga classes. She *loves* the balance poses. I don't think I've seen you in class before. Are you new?"

"Yes, my family just joined this week. This is our first time here," Amy replied.

"Well then, welcome. I've been a member for years and really like it. Those your kids?" Michelle asked.

"Yes, they are," Amy replied.

"They're adorable. And very well behaved," said Michelle. It was true.

"Thank you." Amy beamed.

"Word to the wise," said Michelle. "This is the women's locker room. Kids aren't supposed to be in here. There's a girl's locker room next door where you can have girls of any age and boys who are younger than six. I think that's where you'd want to be when you've got your kids along."

"Oh, thank you. I had no idea. We were going to go on a tour before yoga class but we didn't make it on time. Kids, you know."

"No problem. Some people are really sticklers about the rules so I wanted to make sure you were aware."

"Great to know—and great meeting you. I'm sure I'll see you in Beth's class soon. Thanks again," Amy said as she gathered her children and left the locker room.

The woman who had been glaring at Amy and her kids stepped forward and spoke to Michelle. "I was going to say something about those kids too, but you beat me to it. And you said it so much more diplomatically than I would have. Thank you."

This interchange has all of the characteristics of a well-executed conversation on a difficult topic. In fact, Amy, the rule breaker, *thanked* Michelle as the conversation concluded, as did the onlooker. As you will soon learn, the very words you choose to begin the conversation will not only set the tone but create a sense of freedom for your partner. With a successful opening, you may just find them thanking *you* at the end of the conversation.

As we learned in Chapter 1, defensiveness and the associated stress hormones hamper the neocortex's ability to reason (not to mention shutting down the prefrontal cortex—goodbye, critical thinking!). It is imperative then, to open conversations in a manner that does not provoke defensiveness. You want your partner to be prepared to listen well so they can understand you fully. This chapter explains, step by step, how to ensure that.

This chapter is about openings. It first explains why it is critical to keep the other person from becoming defensive at the outset of a conversation, and why some popular methods of holding difficult conversations, commonly touted as useful, don't actually work well. We will then examine how specific vocabulary choices create a productive dialogue where all parties can bring their best thinking forward. Finally, the chapter provides a concrete methodology for opening conversations—virtually guaranteed to keep defenses low.

KEEPING DEFENSIVENESS LOW

As we learned in Chapter 2, when the human body gets defensive, a hormonal reaction hampers the neocortex and the prefrontal cortex's ability to reason, think critically, and be rational. It is nearly impossible to develop creative solutions when you go up the arousal continuum to the point that the prefrontal cortex begins to shut down. Thus, it is critical to open conversations in a way that does not provoke defensiveness. If the other person becomes defensive, they will not be able to listen, reason, or comprehend to the best of their ability. Nor will they be able to use their creativity and innovation to solve the problem at hand and reach agreement.

The human brain loves order and consistency. Whenever new information is presented that conflicts with status-quo knowledge, beliefs, and attitudes, the brain invokes a level of high alertness that can easily escalate into defensiveness, especially when left unmanaged. When a person hears a bump in the night, for example, they involuntarily enter into "high alert," or alarm on the arousal continuum, until the noise is sorted out and understood. Only then can they become relaxed enough to fall back asleep.

When people encounter new information that makes them feel uncomfortable, the brain automatically invokes this same high alert state. This state leaves your mind predominantly "reactive," operating in a stimulus-response mode. Your reactions are automatic and possibly not what you would choose if you were calmer.

Recall from Chapter 2 that when this happens, you have literally no choice but to behave defensively. The autonomic nervous system governs the process. Even when the threat has passed, the stress hormones may take several minutes to several hours to dissipate from the bloodstream.

It may be easier to be compassionate and understanding about another person's defensiveness once you realize it's an automatic response. To a large extent, that person's reaction is beyond their control, especially if they are not aware of the body's defensive response. This is precisely why it is imperative to open the conversation well.

Intention Versus Impact

A defensive reaction in a conversation can occur regardless of what you *intended* to happen. You may feel like you've just said the most innocuous thing. You might be surprised at the other person's reaction, not understanding why they are upset. This is a case of classic misunderstanding and can easily be corrected provided you quickly realize that the *intention* and *impact* of your communication were actually quite different. With quick thinking and responsiveness, you can repair the conversation and the other person's fight or flight state will likely dissipate quickly.

When your partner is in a state of fear, the executive functions of the brain which control higher order thinking are, for the most part, inaccessible. Some of those functions include the ability to reason, make sense of ideas and behavior, moderate and regulate emotions, accurately assess risk, think critically and creatively, ask for help, self-reflect, and make plans. If you are going to discuss an important topic with a colleague, do you want them in a state where they can't access those functions? Of course not. If they were in such a state, there would be little chance of truly connecting or creating meaning and finding solutions together.

KEEPING DEFENSIVENESS AT BAY

When one person gets defensive, the other person often gets defensive as well. It looks something like this situation:

Lauren and Sam are managers in an in-house creative agency for a large company. They are discussing a high-profile project.

Lauren: We need to send this to an outside agency.

Sam: No. Our internal people need to learn how to do this work. This is the perfect opportunity. Defaulting to a private agency every time we have challenging projects doesn't give them a chance to learn and prove themselves. How are they going to pick up any skills? Give them a chance.

Lauren: Well, we've tried in the past and it just hasn't worked out. I'm not willing to "give your people a chance" on such a high stakes project. We're running a business here, not a design school.

Sam: Stop, stop. Just because you have some "high stakes" project doesn't mean that my people don't get a chance to learn.

Lauren: Actually, it does. Our business lines come first. If your people need some professional development to get them to a competitive level, send them to training. They can't cut their teeth on our top selling product lines!

When she began this conversation, Lauren wasn't necessarily expecting Sam to protest. But by the end they were both defensive. After just a few turns in the conversation, what Lauren thought was a matter of fact request turned into a heated discussion.

This is, in part, the product of our mirror neurons, a special class of brain cells that fire when we observe someone else performing a specific behavior. Italian researchers first discovered mirror neurons in the early 1990s.[17] Researchers implanted electrodes in the brains of several macaque monkeys as part of a research program studying the animal's brain activity while performing various motor actions. One day, one of the researchers reached for his cup of coffee while the monkey was watching him. The electrodes showed that the neurons in the part of the monkey's brain that govern grasping were triggered nearly simultaneously, presumably an involuntary reflex on the part of the monkey's brain. Research over the following decades has uncovered that our own responses to other people's behaviors are not entirely governed by voluntary, logical thought processes either.

Human communication is reciprocal. This major tenet of human communication was documented many decades before the discovery of mirror neurons. In 1975 Charles Berger and Richard Calabrese, researchers at University of California, Davis, published seven axioms of interpersonal communication and uncertainty reduction. Reciprocity was one of them.[18] Human communication behavior is reciprocal and tends to mirror that of those around us.

With both fear and mirror neuron activity being automatic processes, it is no wonder that difficult conversations escalate quickly.

Clearly, starting a conversation in a manner that creates a defensive response does not serve the conversation or any of the parties in it. Let's turn next to some popular methods for holding difficult conversations and examine their usefulness.

I-STATEMENTS AND SANDWICHES

During the morning break of a workshop I was leading, Judy came up to me and asked about "I-statements." She explained, "I was taught years ago to use 'I-statements' when I have something difficult to share, so it doesn't come across as blaming. Instead of starting with 'you,' I start with 'I' to keep them from feeling like I am blaming them for something. Isn't that still the best policy?"

The technique of using "I-statements" has been around since the 1960s, when Dr. Thomas Gordon, a clinical psychologist working with children, promoted it as an effective way of delivering difficult news assertively and without putting the listener on the defensive.[19] If one says, "You had twelve typos in the final draft of the marketing copy you submitted," the other person will likely feel the need to defend themselves. "I was in a hurry." Or: "It was an impossible deadline. I'd like to see you do it with fewer errors under such a tight timeline." On the other hand, an I-statement would be worded as follows: "I found twelve typos in the final draft of the marketing copy you submitted."

Like Judy, you may, in the past, have been told to use I-statements when beginning difficult conversations. For example, "I am concerned that your attire is too risqué for our clients." But there are problems with this. The I-statement focuses on the person initiating the conversation, not on the person being spoken to. It's an approach that intentionally redirects responsibility and ownership to the speaker—and as a result, it lets the offender off the hook. Furthermore, the I-statement does not always focus on the facts but on *interpretation* of the facts. If you initiated the conversation, the emphasis falls on *your* interpretation of how risqué said clothing appears, as well as *your* norms as to the generally accepted level of professionalism for office attire.

This is not to say that I-statements are never appropriate or useful. They're best used in areas where there is far more subjectivity, such as parenting and romantic relationships. The I-statement technique is especially useful when talking with children, as Dr. Gordon first intended. It effectively pairs emotion with a situation and works particularly well to explain an emotional response to a fact or set of facts. For example, when talking to my young daughter I might say, "I'm upset that I've had to tell you three times to brush your hair. We need to leave for school." In the workplace, however, the focus should be on facts, not emotions.

Another methodology that I am regularly asked about is the "sandwich method." In the sandwich method, the person initiating the difficult conversation first says something nice (or innocuous); follows it with the substantial critique (the sandwich filling); and then caps off their remarks with another positive comment. It might go something like this: "Ben, congratulations closing the sale with that latest client. That is a big account and it really makes a difference for our end-of-quarter numbers. We do need to discuss your expense account, however. In courting this client, the expenses exceeded typical allocations by more than 25%. That doesn't set a good example for our newer sales associates and it doesn't sit well upstairs. You've got some other great leads in the hopper. I'm excited to see which of those clients you land next."

The biggest issue (and there are several!) with the sandwich method is that the critical information is lost in the sandwich of positive comments. If the objective is to have a discussion about Ben's expense account, show Ben the respect he deserves by taking the time to actually focus on this topic. Get into the specifics of the situation, sharing with Ben the actual financial data that was out of bounds. Ideally, too, this conversation should have been initiated when Ben's expenses on the account began to bump up against the upper limit of what is acceptable rather than waiting until senior management has noticed and become upset about it.

Another issue with this method is that Ben may not fully comprehend the severity of the situation. He may leave the conversation and discus it with another colleague saying, "My manager is psyched that I closed that great account. Made his end-of-quarter numbers look great. Upstairs noticed that I spent a little more to reel them in but it doesn't seem to be a big deal."

Further, Ben may know on a gut level that something is wrong. Whether he articulates it or not, Ben may feel uneasy because he senses his boss wasn't completely straight with him. That erodes trust. When the critical feedback is literally sandwiched between other, innocuous comments, it is ambiguous at best and damaging at worst. As I am fond of saying, leave the sandwiches for the buffet table and take your difficult conversations straight up.

WORDS CREATE REALITY

Three umpires were talking shop over a beer one evening, discussing how they call balls and strikes. There were some notale differences in their perspectives. The first umpire said, "I calls 'em as they is." The second umpire said, "I calls 'em as I sees 'em." The third, and cleverest, umpire said, "They ain't nothin' til I calls 'em."

We can learn from the ways these three people see the world. The first umpire sees an objective reality that is "out there"; it is his job to apply established labels to what he sees. The second umpire views a more subjective reality and acknowledges that perception plays a role in the matter. The third umpire, however, understands that reality is constructed through the language used to label things, namely balls and strikes.

Most Americans have been to a baseball game and seen a pitch come across the plate differently than how the umpire called it. But the umpire's decision is what goes down in the statistics. The game he describes is the one that exists.

In conversations, too, the words we choose shape reality. They influence not only the outcome but also the reality that is experienced by our conversational partners. What do I mean by that? Every single time we speak, we are creating an experience for the other person—and an experience for ourselves as well. Imagine someone walking into a colleague's office and saying, "I learned at a young age to pick my battles carefully," before launching into a difficult subject. The speaker is labeling the situation, the upcoming conversation, as a battle. Is this opening likely to make the person defensive? Absolutely. What else does one do in a battle but anticipate being attacked, defend oneself, and attack back?

Alternatively, the speaker could say, "I've got a sensitive issue to discuss with you. Is now a good time?" This is a better approach, but there is still room for improvement. When an issue or situation is labeled as "sensitive" most people will jump to the conclusion that something is wrong and that they might be blamed for it. It's a short leap for the brain (remember, the brain is always sensing stimuli, on the lookout for danger—that's its job) to imagine possible scenarios in which an attack will come next. And of course, after an attack comes the involuntary need to defend oneself.

We need to consciously create a shared space in which neither party feels attacked. This requires using language that does not provoke defensiveness. What we choose to call things matters a great deal.

Consider the language that some retailers use to refer to their staff and their customers. At Walmart—and other stores including Family Dollar, Aldi, and Publix—the employees are known as Associates. A term that was once reserved for attorneys and sales roles, "Associate" creates a reality (or attempts to) that the staff members are held in high esteem by the corporation and are peers to management-level employees. "Associate" suggests a business relationship as well—maybe even one in which the employee has a financial stake or partnership in the business.

Another major retailer, Target, calls its customers "Guests." Again, this creates a particular reality for both the "Guests" and the employees, who are incidentally called "Team Members." How you choose to treat a Guest may be significantly different from how you treat a customer. In the same way guests are invited into our homes and treated with care, so too are the guests at Target expected to be hosted by the Team Members. And with a name like Team Members (even at the corporate headquarters, not just in the retail stores), the expectation is clear that teamwork is inherent in the work and highly valued. Employees are not merely running cash registers and restocking shelves, writing marketing plans and developing software. They are playing a specific role on a team that aims to accomplish a larger goal.

When we understand our influence on how reality is constructed through language, we begin to sense how much power we have. This changes how we open conversations on difficult topics. Recall the women in the locker room from the beginning of the chapter.

The topic was difficult but the words that Michelle selected made the conversation friendly. Like Michelle, we can carefully select words and phrases that carry the meaning and nuance most appropriate and strategic to the outcome we desire. Namely, reaching agreement. Rather than laying the lines for a battle, we can build the foundation for a productive discussion that takes both parties' needs into consideration.

When we begin with an intentionally crafted opening, using words selected to create a particular reality, we are more likely to succeed in opening the conversation without making the other person defensive. The next section offers a specific methodology that will help you accomplish this important objective every time.

THE "FACT AND . . ." MODEL

Imagine this scenario:

Emily steps into her boss's office. "Steve is getting all the good travel opportunities," she begins. "You give him all the interesting projects and I get what's left over and I'm so frustrated I'm about ready to quit."

Phil, her boss, is caught off guard. Emily is typically a team player and has always been a good sport about the project assignments she is given. She is a natural with mid-market clients and, as a consequence, is more apt to be sent to Sandusky than to San Francisco. Technically, she is right. Steve does get the better travel opportunities. Phil is inclined to agree with her on that point, but because her demeanor is so aggressive and blaming, he is having a hard time being anything but defensive himself.

If Emily had used the Fact AND model for opening this same conversation, it might have gone something like this:

"Phil, you know I enjoy the travel of this job and you know it's one of the things I love about working here. I absolutely love being on-site with our clients and helping them in person. And my accounts are typically located in smaller cities like Toledo and Tulsa. I'd like a chance to work on some of the accounts in larger cities like Dallas and Detroit. I have to admit that I've been concerned about this for a while. It's really affecting my satisfaction with my job. I've even been looking a little bit for a new job. I could have come to you with it sooner and I didn't, so I'm partly at fault for the situation getting this bad."

In the first scenario, Phil has nowhere to go but to defensiveness. Emily comes out swinging with accusations, blame, and threats. In the second scenario, Emily shares the same information but in a manner that will make Phil more likely to help her—by following the Fact AND model.

The Fact AND model, much like its name suggests, begins with a fact that is generally agreeable to both parties. That fact is connected with another fact using the word "and." Emily starts with the fact that she enjoys the travel in her job. This is something presumably Phil knows, and we expect he would agree with this information, maybe even nodding his head. She has passed the first step of opening without defensiveness: begin with an agreeable fact.

The next step is to add on another agreeable fact. In our example, Emily adds that she loves being onsite with clients and helping them. Repeat the process, adding more facts and getting closer to the "area of impact" as Emily does as she notes the cities in which some of her clients are located. The area of impact is the last thing that is shared; it is the thing that's bugging you, the problem, the issue at hand. Emily connects the area of impact without negating any of what she's just said. It all flows together agreeably.

By building a fact set that leads to the area of impact, you guide the other person into a conversation where you can, together, critically examine the issue using all of your faculties and without becoming defensive. The Fact AND methodology will keep the person in an open and curious state of mind rather than pushing them into fight or flight. They will be able to use their prefrontal cortex and their neocortex, bringing their best listening and critical thinking skills to the conversation.

Let's take a closer look at the methodology and the rationale for each part of the process.

As explained above, we start with an agreeable fact or shared opinion. It must be a suitable premise for the discussion, however. For example, "Jessica, those are beautiful earrings" is not suitable for a conversation about someone's tardiness to work. Neither is "Jessica, you are five-foot seven." These opinions and facts don't relate to the issue at hand.

In selecting an agreeable and germane fact, we begin in a way that arouses, but does not alarm, the other person. We've started from a basis of agreement. Our conversational partner is not defensive. Rather, on the arousal continuum, they may move from calm to aroused but not to fear or terror. Note that you may substitute beliefs, values, and strongly held opinions for facts, provided that they are agreeable to both parties. For example, you might start a conversation with a colleague in which you are think they are not pulling their weight on the project by saying, "The deadlines on this project are intense." While this is not a hard fact, it is a strongly held opinion that you both presumably share.

Next, we use "and" to connect subsequent facts. While I stress the AND in the model (fact AND fact AND fact AND fact AND . . .), the meaning of AND can be conveyed a number of ways, linguistically speaking. Of course, there is the straightforward "and" as in "Phil, you know I enjoy the travel of this job **and** you know it's one of the things I love about working here." (Emphasis is added for your attention and should not be applied in an actual conversation.) AND can also be accomplished with a short pause, the equivalent of the period at the end of a sentence, as in "it's one of the things I love about working here. I absolutely love being on-site with our clients and helping them in person." If I could bold an empty space, I would—the pause between the two sentences serves as a silent AND and continues connecting the facts.

I refer to AND in this model as the Grand AND because of its importance. It is critical to the process.

AND is a conjunction. The function of a conjunction is to connect things. AND is doing precisely that: joining the facts in the set together. The ANDs build relationships between each fact and they build agreement.

It is critical that AND or its silent equivalent, the pause, be used throughout the opening of the conversation. Left unchecked, most people will use "but," another conjunction, or "however," a conjunctive adverb, when bridging from the last fact to the impact. These words disrupt the agreement you've developed. "But" connects through contrast, suggesting "with the exception of." "However" does much the same.

The Fact AND model creates agreement in the mind of your conversational partner as you build your fact set. To disrupt that agreement with "but" or "however" diminishes the chances of a successful conversation. Linguistically, whatever comes after but or however in a series (in this case, a series of facts or mutually held opinions) is different from what came before it. If your listener is agreeing with you and then you use but or however, it is a signal to the brain to disagree with what comes next—before they've even heard what it is!

Just look at how the above example would be different if "however" or "but" were used to connect the area of impact to the fact set rather than AND:

"Phil, you know I enjoy the travel of this job and you know it's one of the things I love about working here. I absolutely love being on-site with our clients and helping them in person. My accounts are typically located in smaller cities like Toledo and Tulsa. However, I'd like a chance to work on some of the accounts in larger cities like Dallas and Detroit."

Listen closely to what's occurring in this version. Fact (I enjoy the travel) AND fact (travel is one of the things I love about working here) AND fact (I love being on-site with clients) AND fact (accounts are located in smaller cities) HOWEVER (I'd like a chance to work in larger cities). By using "however" in making her case, Emily destroyed the agreement she's worked so hard to build. Rather, if she connects instead with AND, the agreement remains intact and Phil is less likely to get defensive.

As you build your fact set, you'll eventually arrive at the area of impact. This is the reason for having the conversation. Think of it not as a problem, however, but as simply the next (and final) fact in the set you've just laid out. Alternatively, you could think of it as the conclusion to the fact set you've just laid out; the final AND could be replaced with "as a result."

Once you have laid out your fact set and the impact, all connected with ANDs, the next step is to stop talking. Yep. Shush. Count to ten in your head if you have to. Or twenty. If you've successfully opened the conversation without defensiveness, your partner is thinking at this point, considering what's been said so far. That's exactly where you want them. Congratulations, the most challenging part is complete. The conversation is not yet over, though. You've still got some work to do.

And Then It Got Very Quiet

Let's suppose Emily followed the Fact AND model and concluded her thoughts. Phil had been nodding as if in silent agreement. At the completion of her fact set, she was quiet. But the silence felt disturbing and uncomfortable. Emily got a little nervous. She was about to say something but then she remembered that some quiet is okay. A good thing even.

Many people feel this same discomfort with silence. This silence is critical, however. When people give in to the discomfort and say something, they will often either recant or justify, both of which work in disservice to the opening of the conversation. Recanting— saying something such as "Well, it's really not that important, don't worry about it, I'm probably overreacting"—minimizes the area of impact and damages your credibility. Your facts were compelling and interesting. The area of impact sounded significant. Now you're backpedaling? That's confusing.

Justifying is equally ineffective, and typically includes adding more information, repeating facts you've already shared, and becoming more entrenched in your position. At least that's how it will come across to your conversational partner. It sounds like this: "Really. Steve *does* get to go to better cities than I do. He does. And there aren't even good restaurants in the cities I go to and the best hotels are these mom and pop places where I don't even get hotel points." Justifying is defensive behavior and it is likely to spur defensive communication behavior from your conversational partner as well. Who, incidentally, was carefully considering your well thought-out fact set before you interrupted him.

The silence marks the end of one way of thinking about something and creates a transitional space where a new beginning can emerge. Dr. William Bridges, a leading researcher on successfully navigating change, aptly labeled this moment as "fertile emptiness."

As Bridges explains in a discussion of transitions and turning points, "Things end, there is a time of fertile emptiness, and then things begin anew."[20] While Bridges was referring to life transitions and turning points such as career decisions, getting married, becoming parents, or the death of a loved one, his framework is equally applicable to transitions in conversations. In fact, many life turning points begin with a conversation—a discussion with a spouse about a job change or starting a new company, a conversation with the person you are dating about spending the rest of your lives together, or talking with an aging parent about ensuring they live out their final years in dignity.

Is the space really empty? From Emily's standpoint, it seems so. There is a temptation to say something, anything. She has just shared important and personal information and in so doing she has made herself vulnerable. But if she can remain grounded during this uncomfortable part of the conversation, the results will outweigh the discomfort.

Because from Phil's vantage point, the emptiness is not, in fact, emptiness at all. Phil is busy thinking and examining the new information Emily shared. He needs time to consider what she said, make sense of it, and integrate it with his own fact set before responding. And he is likely to do this if he has not gotten defensive. Phil may not even have noticed the silence. After all, there is a great deal of activity going on in his mind as he considers Emily's fact set and thinks through his available courses of action and what he might say next.

CONCLUSION

Congratulations! You've successfully completed the second step in facilitating a difficult conversation. You might actually find it's not so difficult after all. In fact, the other person might thank you for the information you've shared, just as Amy, the new member at the YMCA, did with Michelle. You've voiced your concern in a matter of fact manner and given your partner something to think about. They're considering the issue and they are not defensive, so they can bring their best reasoning and critical thinking skills to the conversation. Great work!

It is worth noting that in some cases, despite your best efforts to open the conversation in a manner that does not provoke defensiveness, the person might move rapidly up the arousal continuum to fear and exhibit the corresponding defensiveness anyway. It is important to understand that those with a history of trauma, failure, or humiliation will move up the arousal continuum faster, often in the face of a fairly small challenge or perceived threat. They may also escalate up the continuum if there is an established pattern in which the person typically gets defensive whenever you interact. Regardless of the cause, if the other person gets defensive, it is important to be patient, slow down, and work on building trust.

If defensiveness is running high on either your part or theirs, it is okay to take a break in the conversation if the context allows it. Perhaps not in a meeting with many people, but if it is just two of you, it is okay to suggest you revisit the topic later in the day or at another time. This will provide an opportunity for stress hormones to dissipate and will give a fresh start to the conversation. Sometimes a break, even as little as five minutes, can have a measurable impact on reducing defensiveness.

So far, we have presumed that you have control over how and when the conversation begins. We looked at the conversation from the perspective of you initiating it. If the difficult conversation finds you and you are not the one who initiated it however, it may not have been started in a way designed to keep *you* from getting defensive. In fact, you might find yourself feeling incredibly defensive at the outset. If this is the case, recall the techniques from the last chapter on staying calm. Those techniques will help you stay on the lower end of the arousal continuum where you will be better able to regulate your emotions and your thoughts.

In the next chapter, we look at what to do after the conversation has begun. But first, complete the exercises at the end of the chapter to gain mastery over opening conversations without making the other person defensive.

EXERCISES

#9: How Not to Start a Conversation

Starting a conversation in a manner that makes the other person defensive will never yield positive results. Some examples of poor ways to begin a conversation on a difficult topic include:

"We need to talk."

"I've got a serious matter to discuss with you."

"I learned to pick my battles at a young age."

Listen closely during the coming week and jot down any other opening lines that made you or others feel defensive.

#10: Use the Fact AND model

Use the Fact AND model to develop a list of facts for your next difficult conversation. Note that you do not need to use exactly five facts to tee up your conversation. Use as many as makes sense in order to introduce the topic and reach the area of impact.

Come back to this formula when you are preparing for difficult conversations in the future.

Fact:

Fact:

Fact:

Fact:

Fact:

Impact:

CHAPTER 6

Listen and Learn

I was recently visiting with another consultant who, like me, works to improve workplace culture. As we shared our approaches, I mentioned listening as a key pillar of my work. "Really?" he responded. "Don't people already know how to listen?" he asked.

I asked him, in turn, to share a time when he felt that he and another person were in sync on something.

"Oh, that's easy. Yesterday. My business partner and I were working on some new concepts. Each idea built on the one before it and we were completely in sync."

"Perfect example," I said. "The two of you were really listening to one another. Now," I continued, "tell me about a time when that didn't happen. Tell me about a time when you and someone were missing each other at every turn."

He was quiet for a moment, then he grew somber. "This morning, and most every day," he said, "with my wife."

"Yeah," I acknowledged. "But what would it be like if she listened to you like your business partner does? And you listened to her that way, too?"

"Okay," he said. "I see the need for listening."

Listening is a crucial component of effective conversations, difficult or otherwise. Listening to what is said and what is left unsaid is critical, and as we learned earlier, listening is severely hampered when defenses are heightened. The further up the arousal continuum we move, the less ability we have to listen and think critically. In this chapter, we look at two important concepts related to becoming a better listener in a difficult conversation: adaptive listening, or how to listen while you speak, and objective inquiry, or the art of getting curious and asking questions.

ADAPTIVE LISTENING

Shannon, a project manager, was holding an emergency meeting. There was a very real possibility that the timeline on a critical project she was managing would slip if the team didn't meet their next milestone. And it wasn't looking good. Shannon knew that if the team addressed this situation head on, there was a strong chance they could get the project back on schedule, and consequently, within budget.

She convened the key stakeholders around a conference room table and laid out the current situation. As she spoke, Shannon was acutely aware of the tension in the room. She made eye contact with everyone in the room in turn and observed carefully to see who was in agreement, who was confused or had questions, and any other reactions she could discern.

When she saw puzzlement or confusion, she shared more details on the point she was currently discussing. She slowed her rate of speech slightly and sometimes stopped to ask specifically if there were questions before moving to the next point.

Shannon exhibited a high level of social sensitivity and emotional intelligence throughout the meeting, focusing on her audience and their reactions to her message as much as she focused on her message. Shannon was in a highly orchestrated and expertly maneuvered dance with her audience that I call adaptive listening. She was adapting as she delivered her message, sometimes slightly, sometimes massively, in response to the audience's reaction. In so doing, she was listening intently to her audience, even though *she* was the one doing the speaking.

Adaptive listening occurs when you are speaking, not when you are in typical "listening" mode. We often think of listening as the thing we are doing when it is not our turn to talk in the conversation. While that is certainly a common form of listening, conversations on difficult topics require just as much, if not more, listening while speaking, or adaptive listening. When we focus in equal measure on the message and how the audience is receiving the message, we can better tailor our approach to meet their needs in the moment. In any conversation where there is true dialogue, you are both the speaker and the listener, alternately and simultaneously. As you talk, you read the response of your partner and adjust your message or approach accordingly.*

Adaptive listening is both a science and an art. It is a spontaneous adaptation of the delivery of your message. Your overall message does not change. Your commitment and conviction, your research and supporting data, the substance of your message, does not waver. Rather, what does change is your delivery, your word choice, your rhythm. As you listen while you speak and sense where your audience needs more, or less, you adapt to their goals, values,

---

*I borrowed and modified this term from "listener adaptation," a phrase which describes how non-native speakers of a language adapt their dialect to become more like the dialect of the native speakers of that language. As a result, they are more intelligible to the native speakers.

and beliefs. Adaptive listening enables you to remain present and fully engaged in the conversation and it also lessens the possibility that your listeners will miss important details, stated or unstated.

Your presence and dedication to the conversation and, accordingly, to the other person, bring with them respect and trust. When we are taking a careful read of our audience as we speak to them, they will sense that we are right there, in that moment, with them and only them. This shows tremendous respect for the other person. That we can be free from distractions and place our focus on this moment, on this conversation, means we are paying them the honor of our undivided attention. Such respect builds trust.

Adaptive listening preempts misunderstanding. Misunderstandings occur when there is confusion, disagreement, or other inability to create shared meaning. When you are practicing adaptive listening, you become aware of the cues that indicate any such confusion or lack of shared meaning and you are able to address it in the moment. In this way, the conversation is improvisational, much like jazz music.

Whether speaking with one person, with a team as Shannon was, or with a large audience, adaptive listening will bring you closer to your audience and will be formative in earning their trust.

For some, adaptive listening comes quite naturally. For others, the skill can be developed. To increase your ability to listen while speaking, you must first bring your attention to the listener. We will presume that you are unequivocally comfortable with and knowledgeable about the content you are sharing. If that is not the case, get crystal clear on your message and any supporting details that may be required in sharing your message. This is paramount.

In honing your skill at adaptive listening, I suggest a three-part process. First, with message firmly in place, draw your attention to your listener's body language. This is an especially useful place to start if you are in an uncomfortable situation (i.e., a conversation on a difficult topic or speaking to a large audience). You will be able to detect interest as your audience moves while you speak. When you detect them leaning forward, it is an indication of interest. They might lean slightly to one side rather than forward. This also indicates listening and interest. Listeners may also tilt their head slightly to one side or nod subtly as they listen carefully and consider what you are saying.

When you notice your listener leaning back, the information may be redundant or not of interest to them. They are not listening as closely. Other indications of not listening may be obvious to some but are worth mentioning here nonetheless: shaking of the head (which may also mean disagreement), fidgeting, looking at a watch or clock or using a smartphone—and not to take notes on what you are saying but instead to check email, text, or other activity unrelated to the discussion at hand.

Watch also for the general openness or closedness of their body. A closed body with arms crossed is a general indication of disagreement. If shoulders are rounded or the person is making themselves look small, it may indicate defensiveness or fear. An open body posture on the other hand, generally indicates agreement or alignment.

Once you are comfortable reading the general body language of others, the next area to on which to concentrate is facial expression. Facial expressions that indicate interest and agreement generally include smiles (large or small), animated appearance (positive), mirroring of your own facial expressions, and holding your gaze. Additionally, a slight frown or pursed lips may indicate a sign of thoughtful consideration. The listener in this case may be integrating or comparing information that you are sharing with other knowledge, beliefs, or opinions.

Facial expressions indicating disagreement or confusion include obvious frowns, lips pressed tightly together, or a raised chin. A knit brow likely indicates confusion or questions. However, like a slight frown, a slightly knit brow may indicate consideration and contemplation. Taking into account other non-verbal cues may help corroborate whether the knit brow indicates thinking or confusion.

The specific combination of knit brow, lips pressed tightly together, and chin raised was recently identified as the "not" expression, indicating anger, disgust, and contempt.[21] As in, "I do NOT agree with what's being said in any way, shape or form."

Eye contact also provides insight into your audience's state of listening. Indications that your audience is not listening or is perhaps disagreeing with you include downcast eyes or not making direct eye contact, actively seeking eye contact from others to exchange a knowing glance (one of skepticism rather than agreement), and eyes closed. And here we're talking about sleeping rather than being deep in meditative thought over your brilliance!

Note that some people are naturally far more non-verbally expressive than others. The more you come to know your audience, whether it is an individual, a team, or a large group, the more you will come to understand how closely they parallel the general guidelines offered here.

It is worth mentioning that these factors generally represent American/Western culture (although the researchers who identified the "not" face studied people from many different cultures and found the "not" face to transcend cultures). Other cultures may vary considerably in their non-verbal norms and associated meanings. This is particularly true for eye contact.

I recommend practicing and sharpening this skill in low-stakes conversations initially, for obvious reasons. When you are in a high-stakes conversation (conversation on a challenging topic, presentation to senior executives, etc.), you may be nervous. If you have honed your adaptive listening skills in situations that are less intense, they will begin to come second nature to you when you are in the high-stakes conversations.

It is also easier for your brain to learn a new skill when you are in a less stressful situation. With less cognitive load, you will have more bandwidth available to use in the development of the new skill. When you are in a high-stakes conversation, it makes sense to bring all of your faculties to the content of that conversation. Of course, it is more important than ever to connect with your audience in those high-stakes conversations, so start practicing now!

Because there are cultural and individual variances, on occasion you may not be sure how to read the nonverbal cues of others. In those instances, the best thing to do is ask. "I'm sensing some confusion and I'd like to stop at this point and check in before I go any further." Or perhaps, "I get the feeling we might not all be on the same page. I'd like to take the pulse of the group before moving on." Invitations like these offer an audience, whether a single individual or a larger group, a practical and meaningful way into the conversation and are particularly helpful if you are unsure of what your adaptive listening is telling you.

Next, we will look at the natural extension of your adaptive listening: getting curious and asking questions to learn more about the other person's perspective.

OBJECTIVE INQUIRY

Danielle, an aquatics director at a municipal recreation and fitness center, was frustrated with one of the community members. Iris, a long-time member of the rec center and pool, was upset about recent schedule changes to the aqua-aerobics program designed specifically for senior citizens. She had been calling regularly to complain to Danielle. "She calls so often! And sometimes she even tries to disguise her voice to make it sound like more people are upset than just her, but I can always tell it's her from the caller ID," Danielle lamented. "How can I get her to stop calling me?"

"What do you say when she calls?" I asked.

"I tell her that I'm so sorry and that it wasn't my decision to change the schedule. It's because the high school started sharing the pool with us so they can have a swim team. I pretty much say the same thing every time. I try my best to be apologetic but it's not working," Danielle replied.

The missing piece here is to consider the impact on Iris and what the schedule change means to her. Danielle's response doesn't include Iris. I advised Danielle to get curious, really curious, about Iris's concerns the next time she called. Danielle reported back to me several days later. She shared this:

"Iris called again and this time I asked her about her life and how the schedule change affected her. She said, 'Danielle, we seniors are some of the most over-scheduled people on the planet. I probably have too much going on and I know that. But aqua-aerobics is important for my health. My doctor says I need to do low-impact exercise and this class is exactly that. Plus, I've made some new friends in the class so I love going. But at 8:30 on Thursdays, your new time for the class, is when I meet my three best girlfriends from high school. Danielle, I'm 81 years old. For the better part of the past 63 years, my girlfriends and I have been meeting at Denny's for breakfast at 8:30 on Thursdays. My friends are just as over-scheduled as I am, so I can't ask them to change the time we meet for breakfast.'"

With a little bit of well-intentioned curiosity, Danielle was able to ask the right questions and get to the real issue with Iris. And as you might guess, Iris felt heard by Danielle and no longer needed to call to complain. Danielle certainly wasn't able to solve the situation for Iris or make a change to the schedule, but Iris was no longer struggling to make her views known.

When we express real curiosity in our conversations with others, especially when we have to discuss difficult topics, we can learn new information that might enable us to see the situation differently and, accordingly, respond differently. That same curiosity can make a world of difference to the person you are speaking with. As with Iris, the person may feel heard and understood in far deeper ways than they felt before you became curious.

When we can authentically tap into our curiosity, we can ask questions from a place I refer to as objective inquiry. Objective inquiry does not have a specific agenda. The questions are not leading questions; they are not designed to influence the other person's thinking or behavior. Rather they are, as the name suggests, objective. They are not influenced by personal feelings. They are not influenced by opinions. Instead, they are designed to get at a set of facts, the facts that the other person holds.

Connecting with the part of you that holds the keys to your innate curiosity requires setting judgment aside so curiosity can flourish. When judgment begins to crowd your thoughts, it squelches curiosity. Your mind cannot be simultaneously judging and curious about the same thing.

Quite often in difficult situations, both parties are operating with different, and incomplete, fact sets. When we engage in objective inquiry and ask questions from a place of curiosity, we stand a chance at shedding light on our partner's fact set. While I call them "facts" here, this "fact set" may also include the other person's opinions, beliefs, and theories about the situation. Whether they are facts or opinions, they exist and they have a bearing on the situation at hand.

Only when we get to an authentically curious place can we tap into the power of objective inquiry. In some situations, you may need to look very deep within to find the place from which you can be organically curious. If your curiosity is forced, insincere, or disingenuous, it may do more harm than good.† Human beings have finely tuned BS detectors. We can smell it a long way off. If a line of questioning is inauthentic or manipulative the other person will likely sense it and it will erode trust and respect. On the other hand, when questions come from an honorable and curious vantage point, they work to build trust and respect.

In some situations, where the other person's actions or point of view seem so strange and bizarre and perhaps not grounded in the same reality that you experience on a daily basis, I am fond of asking myself this question: "On what planet or in what alternate universe does this person's point of view make sense or hold up to reason?" This question is designed to shake up your thinking and get you to see their side, and from there, formulate a question to ask. This is a question for you to consider silently and is not, in any case *ever*, a question for you to ask in your "outside voice."

CONCLUSION

In this chapter we have covered how to listen in a new way and how to be curious about the other person's perspective. Continue to

---

†If you have trouble feeling respect for the person you are addressing, they will be able to sense it. You may need to look outside their current role to find a place where you have organic respect for the person. If you are stuck, look to areas of similarity you share with the other person or things you can relate to. "He has aging parents just like I do," or "He's a dog owner and I like dogs." Even if it is a relatively minor thing, it will provide a basis for developing authentic respect.

practice the skills of adaptive listening and objective inquiry by completing the exercises at the end of this chapter.

At this point, you now have the knowledge to work through a conversation on a difficult topic by preparing emotionally, opening that conversation in a manner that doesn't create defensiveness, and listening in a mode that demonstrates both your respect and trust for the other person even when you are the one doing the talking. You are curious and asking questions from an objective stance rather than presuming or predicting outcomes, and in so doing, getting more facts on the table. The next step is to move beyond the two of you to a larger context and identify others who may be affected by the situation.

EXERCISES

#11: Adaptive Listening

Adaptive listening is the process of listening and speaking simultaneously, and in that listening, dynamically adapting the message to meet the real-time needs of the audience.

It is a spontaneous dance in which you adapt the delivery of the message to meet your audience where they are. Your overall message does not change. What *does* change is your delivery, your word choice, your rhythm.

Adaptive listening occurs when you are speaking, not when you are in typical "listening" mode.

List several people you know who seem to have this skill. What do they specifically do that exhibits characteristics of adaptive listening?

#12: Getting Curious in Difficult Conversations

Think specifically about a difficult conversation you are preparing to hold.

Write out 10–15 questions you could ask in the course of that conversation. What are the things you don't know that might make a difference to help you understand the other person's perspective?

CHAPTER 7

Beyond Your Story

Stephanie, a team lead in a large technology company, and her team member Justin didn't see eye to eye on much. Stephanie consequently implemented the advice she'd been raised on: if you don't have anything nice to say, don't say anything at all. Accordingly, she limited her contact with Justin, often avoiding him and interacting with others on the team instead.

Unfortunately, other team members weren't as well equipped to provide what she needed. Many times, those colleagues had to go to Justin to get the answers to the questions Stephanie posed. Justin played his part too, firing sarcastic comments at Stephanie during team meetings and adamantly disagreeing with her whenever an opportunity arose.

You've probably heard the maxim "there are two sides to every story." I'm about to suggest that there are far more than two sides to any story and at a minimum you should be considering three stories, or sides to the story, in every difficult situation. When we move beyond our own story and the story of our counterpart, we begin to see a more nuanced, complex situation. Myriad other people and situations may be affected by this one set of circumstances. Acknowledgement of the stories of those people and perspectives may be the motivation that we need to see a different, and sometimes more important, viewpoint. Let's take a look at the various stories in this situation, including Stephanie's and Justin's.

THE ROLE OF HISTORY

Stephanie's story: Stephanie knows that two years ago Justin also applied for the lead role that she now holds. She recalled being a confederate in Justin's sarcastic, witty comments back then. But ever since she got the lead developer role, he has been a thorn in her side. So she steers clear at every turn.

Justin's story: Justin feels his management team made a big mistake in promoting Stephanie instead of him. He had more seniority and his technical knowledge surpassed Stephanie's. Stephanie even admitted to that. Justin knows that eventually the management team will see the error of their ways and give him the lead role he so rightly deserves.

Their co-workers' stories: Janet, a developer in her late 50s, is hoping she'll be offered an early retirement package. As much as she loves her job, she detests the way Stephanie and Justin treat each other. Jamal, an eager developer just out of college, keeps his head down and tries not to get mixed up in the cross-fire. He knows there's something going on between these two, but he isn't sure what and he doesn't want to get involved. Fredrick, the admin who supports their whole floor, rolls his eyes whenever he sees either of them coming. They both like to vent to Fredrick and he has a hard time listening to either one of them.

Their manager's story: With the immature behavior coming from both Stephanie and Justin, their boss Jack is wondering if he made the right choice in promoting Stephanie, and he's sure glad he didn't select Justin. With all the complaints he gets from others on the team—even the admin has approached him about this—he's frustrated and somewhat disgusted. He knows the team isn't operating at full capacity because of Stephanie and Justin's pettiness.

There are many directions we can turn our lens to see a different side to the story. We could look beyond Stephanie and Justin's colleagues to their friends and family members. It's likely that their conflict at work, however clandestine they might think it is, is being dragged out and paraded around in their personal lives as well. And so we can add the stories of their families and friends.

When either Justin or Stephanie turns their attention to any one of the multitude of stories in their situation and seriously considers it, it will give them pause. When we begin to glimpse the far-ranging effects of our actions, the view can provide motivation for changing our behavior. This is the power of looking at the many stories or perspectives of the situation.

It is common to be stuck in our own story. We human beings are narrative creatures after all. Storytelling is in our very makeup and is what allowed our ancestors to hand down knowledge and culture from generation to generation. We share facts, beliefs, norms, and customs through story. The stories take on a life of their own, reinforcing the key messages. The more the story is repeated, whether to ourselves or to others, the more solidly it becomes entrenched in our mind and in our organization's culture.

We may be prompted, sometimes by the very people we are telling our story to, to consider the other side of the story. For every "Stephanie's side" there is a "Justin's side" and vice versa. But we are not often prompted to examine the full cascade of stories that stem from the initial course of events.

CASE IN POINT

Courtney and Luke, sales colleagues at a large medical device company, were dining in a neighborhood bistro with a potential client. Getting an appointment with this prospect was difficult. Courtney and Luke had been working on this account for close to a year and they finally had a break: Dr. Kumar Patel, the lead urology surgeon, and Barbara Randolph, the chief medical officer, were meeting them for lunch.

As Courtney ordered the grilled ahi tuna sandwich, she asked the server, "The menu says the sandwich comes with piquant sauce, can you describe that for me?"

Amir, the server, responded, "Certainly, it is a spicy aioli sauce, mayonnaise-based, seasoned with Ají Limo, or lemon drop pepper. It's a medium spicy sauce and the slice of avocado that also sits on the sandwich soothes the heat quite nicely. But if you'd like, we can put the piquant sauce on the side."

"It sounds lovely and I enjoy spicy food. I'll take the sandwich, with the sauce," Courtney replied. Amir took the orders from the rest of the group and disappeared into the kitchen.

Once the food arrived, Courtney found, much to her surprise, that her ahi tuna sandwich was also topped with a generous portion of matchstick-cut cucumbers. Cucumbers that were *not* in the description of the sandwich on the menu. Cucumbers were one of the few foods that Courtney did not like.

Courtney struggled to contain her frustration as she called Amir back over to the table. "There was no mention of cucumbers on the menu," she snapped, more sternly than she'd intended. You see, not only did Courtney not like cucumbers, she had a history of asking for dishes to be prepared without cucumbers (when they were listed on the menu!), only to have her requests go unheeded. It took only a mere slice of cucumber on a salad to set her off. The conversation escalated quickly.

Kumar and Barbara traded glances while Courtney exchanged fiery rounds with the server. Luke attempted to divert attention away from Courtney by engaging the doctor and the administrator in a conversation about the weather.

Let's look at the stories in this setting.

Courtney's story: Her story is apparent and in the fore-front of this interaction. What the others in this interaction don't know, however, is her long history of receiving cucumbers when she'd asked for them to be held.

Amir's story: Amir dutifully answered all of Courtney's questions and she'd seemed like a pleasant customer. Given she's obviously on a business luncheon, he is more than a little surprised at her extreme reaction, especially given his attempt to have the sandwich revised to her liking.

Luke's story: He's dined with Courtney countless times and borne witness to her cucumber explosions over the years. He's taken to carefully reading the menu himself when he dines with Courtney, to make sure she hasn't overlooked a cucumber reference. He saw the look exchanged between their potential clients and he's worried that Courtney's outburst might cost them the sale.

Kumar's story: A cucumber lover himself, he's a more than a little put off by Courtney's reaction. Not only does she seem to be overreacting, she's upset about something he loves.

Barbara's story: Courtney's reaction reminds her of another vendor the hospital worked with a few years back. A radiology vendor had a quick temper about many issues and Barbara found him insufferable to work with because of it.

In addition to these five stories, there are also the stories of other diners seated nearby. How this situation is discussed and handled will affect their experience of their own meals. There is also the chef's story. No doubt the chef designed the sandwich with the cucumber matchsticks for a very good reason and he may be frustrated and angry to have to remake the meal for Courtney. Courtney will most certainly be discussed among the servers, prep chefs, and managers, and each of those individuals will have their own stories.

This brief situation effectively illustrates nearly ten different stories represented in a simple interaction between two people in a casual encounter. Each viewpoint, or story, is influenced by the person's history and worldview.

MAKING THE MOST OF OTHER VIEWPOINTS

When we take into account that there are many possible stories, we see the situation differently. One of the ancillary stories might just be the motivation needed to take a difficult situation head on. Likewise, one of the ancillary stories can serve as a way to address the topic so that neither party feels blamed or threatened. Using the Fact AND model introduced earlier in this book coupled with their coworkers' story, an opening to the discussion between Stephanie and Justin might go something like this: "Justin, we don't always see eye to eye. Heck, we rarely see eye to eye. I was thinking about how that comes across to the others on our team and I'll bet it doesn't reflect too favorably on either of us. Maybe we should call a truce before this situation takes the team down."

Going beyond your story requires a certain degree of maturity. Oftentimes in difficult situations we are not always at our most mature. Sometimes we are whiny and immature and just want our own way. We are right and we are righteous and everyone else is wrong (unless they are on our side!). To see the situation from an alternative viewpoint or several alternative viewpoints necessitates letting go of being right and along with it, any righteousness we might feel. In doing so, a space of vulnerability is created that makes it easier for the other person to engage with us in a new way.

When you take the time to explore the stories of those individuals and entities who are connected to the difficult situation while not being immediately party to it, you stand a chance to grow both professionally and personally. When you stop to consider that there are stories beyond the two obvious ones, like your manager's story, the team or department's story, the division or business unit's story, the customers' stories and so on, it is easier to see the broader impact of our words and deeds.

No example better illustrates the power of additional stories to provide perspective and motivation than Nancy's. Nancy waited to speak to me in private after a speaking engagement. She shared this: "Janel, when you talked about there being more than my story and the other person's story, something massively shifted for me. My older sister and I haven't spoken to one another in the past 10 years. It goes way back, obviously, to something that happened a long time ago that was very hurtful. I've always acknowledged there was her side and my side. But today, I saw all the other stories. All the other people in my family who are hurt by our rift. My parents. Oh, it must break their hearts to see their two adult daughters not speaking to one another. I never really got that until today.

And even bigger than the impact on my parents, I think, is the impact on my kids. They aren't getting to know my sister's kids. I'm depriving them of the experience of having cousins. Not to mention what a bad example I'm setting about how to get along with others and the importance of family. It just breaks my heart to see the story from my kids' side. I've never been motivated to try to restore the relationship. I've always thought I'm right and she's wrong—and I know she thinks she's right and I'm wrong—and I've never been able to see beyond that. Today, for the first time ever, I'm motivated to try to restore my relationship with her. I know it won't be easy. But I now see it as far more important than I'd ever thought."

CONCLUSION

We have seen how every situation can be viewed from multiple perspectives and multiple stories can be told. Often the situation is far more nuanced when we take these stories into account. When we take the time to consider all the sides to a story, we may come to very different conclusions than when we consider only our own view and that of the person directly in front of us.

Think of the difficult situations you face. What are the additional stories you haven't considered? Who is affected by the conversations on difficult topics you need to have? Use the exercises at the end of this chapter to identify additional stories of people who are concerned about the difficult situations you face.

EXERCISES

#13: Three Plus Three More

List three sides of a story in a recent or current difficult situation, at home or at work. Jot down as many details as you can think of that characterize these stories.

My story:

Their story:

The third story:

Now list as many additional stories (at least three more!) as you can think of. Jot down as many details as you can think of that characterize those other stories.

Don't worry about getting them in order of importance, etc. Just identify as many as you can.

#14: Research Makes Right

Don't rely on your made-up story. You've done the hard work of identifying who else is affected and in what ways. Now, take the next step and research one or more of those stories. Talk to one or more of the other people involved in the story and find out what the world (and your situation) looks like from their vantage point.

Where does their actual story differ from the one you thought they'd have? Where is it similar?

CHAPTER 8

Reaching Agreement

Anthony, an account manager for a rapidly growing software company, recently learned that one of the company's top clients had been communicating directly with his colleague Eric, the lead software developer on the project. The client had Eric's mobile phone number and was speaking with him regarding software change requests, circumventing the formal process for handling such matters. Many of the requests Eric was readily making for the client were change requests that would typically be vetted by an oversight team and some were changes that would normally involve an upcharge. As Anthony saw it, the company was losing control and losing revenue.

Anthony talked with Eric and explained that it was problematic for him to be working outside the established processes. Eric grew defensive and said that other developers were doing the same thing on some of the other accounts. Further, he argued, going through cumbersome change request processes and involving an account manager and a project manager slowed things down and was too many fingers in the pie. He said to be the great developer that he was, he needed to be closer to the voice of the customer. Literally.

Agreement seemed a long way off.

Agreement is the conclusion you are striving for in a difficult conversation. If total agreement is not possible, you are at least striving for mutual understanding and a shared view of the situation. This chapter looks at how to generate agreement and how to handle situations where agreement feels out of reach, as it inevitably will in some situations.

TYPE 1 OR TYPE 2 AGREEMENT

When agreement can be reached in one conversation, it is what I call Type 1 agreement. Perhaps your employee has been late to work three times in the past two weeks but otherwise has been a dependable and punctual employee. The first time it happened, you didn't mention it. After all, he's been so dependable. Anyone can have a little mishap, right? The second time you thought seriously about bringing it up with your employee, but got distracted by a more important matter. Now it's happened three times—within two weeks—and you're not the kind of person who saves things up and lambasts employees in their annual performance review. So you bring it up. And it is very likely that you can resolve the matter in one conversation. Type 1 agreement.

Other times, it will take two or more conversations to reach agreement. I refer to these situations as Type 2 agreement. Perhaps this isn't the first time you've raised the issue. Maybe it's not even the second or the third. It's the eleventh time you've discussed it . . .

and the behavior hasn't changed. Or maybe it is an issue that has persisted for a long time without anyone addressing it. Or perhaps trust has been broken (or was never established in the first place). Or in still other cases, you may not have respect for the other person. In any of these situations, it will take two or more conversations to ultimately reach agreement.

It is important to note that in a Type 2 situation, you want to start by addressing an appropriately sized portion of the situation (think small). Since it is going to take more than one conversation, there is no rush to solve it all at once. In parsing it out into multiple conversations, you create the opportunity to build trust over time, restore respect, and strengthen the relationship. Follow this four-step process in a Type 2 situation in order to provide structure and end with agreement, each step of the way.

1. Acknowledge the situation. In the case of Nancy from the previous chapter, the woman who is estranged from her sister: "We haven't spoken in ten years."
2. State your motivation to change the situation. "You're my sister and you're important to me."
3. Share your commitment to your motivation. "I'd like to work on restoring our relationship, and I know it might not be easy."
4. Ask for their commitment in return. "Are you in?" If she says yes, that's a great place to end the first conversation. Make a commitment to talk again soon, for example, "I'll see you at mom's birthday dinner in a few weeks and we can spend a little time together then."

It's important to end each of the Type 2 conversations with agreement. It may be helpful to set parameters at the start of the discussion (i.e., "Let's just get caught up on our kids' lives today.") and stick to those parameters. In Nancy's case, it was important to build good will and trust with her sister as a foundation for talking about the pain from the past. Their relationship was not strong enough to start with the hurt from a decade ago. Current events including jobs, news of other family members, and the like are a good place from which to begin to restore the relationship in a situation like Nancy's.

When stepping into a difficult situation or a difficult conversation, carefully consider whether you intend to reach Type 1 or Type 2 agreement and proceed accordingly.

INVENT POSSIBILITIES AND RECIPROCATE

As you move into the agreement phase of the conversation, it is important not to have a fixed, rigid idea of what agreement or a potential solution looks like. It's only an agreement if it feels like everyone wins. To get started, you want to get a number of ideas on the table, some from each person. Invite your counterpart to share a potential solution. Listen closely. Accept the idea. You do not have to place any valuation or valence on the idea (good/bad/neutral), but rather accept that it is an idea. Reciprocate by putting an idea of your own on the table and continue to build ideas in like fashion. Once you have several ideas on the table, then and only then, does it make sense to begin to sort through them.

Mix and mingle the ideas you've generated, seeing if there is a way to combine together parts and pieces that came from each of you. When agreement is reached with both parties feeling that they have contributed to the outcome, the acceptance and buy-in will be higher. It's more likely that the agreement will "stick." Embracing the unknown and letting go of attachment to what the agreement needs to look like will help reach an agreement that has mutual buy-in and acceptance.

THE COST OF DISAGREEMENT

When agreement is elusive, it is easy to say, "Well, I guess we just agree to disagree." When we do this, we leave disagreement as the context for our next conversation with that person. That disagreement hangs in the space like a foul smell, polluting subsequent conversations, even when they are not on the same topic.

The costs of ending a conversation in this manner are steep. First, this is a disrespectful way to end a search for agreement. Presumably, if this is the note the conversation is ending on, the earlier steps outlined in this book have not been followed or if they have, a trigger was hit and either one or both parties have escalated up the arousal continuum and become defensive. Second, this result does not provide latitude for resuming the conversation at a later date, when agreement might be more feasible. Third, this does not bode well for the development of trust between the two parties. There is no give and take, there is no compromise, and there is no possibility for a different outcome.

Let me introduce you to a different way to do disagreement.

DISAGREEMENT WITH POSSIBILITY

Rather than disrespectfully commenting on the disagreement, there is a way to acknowledge the current lack of agreement and leave room for a different outcome. There are three parts to leaving a disagreement with possibility for future agreement.

First, clearly and straightforwardly acknowledge the lack of agreement in the present tense. For example, "We do not agree on an outcome for this situation right now." By specifically stating that you have not reached agreement, you are being straight with the other person. That, by its very nature, is respectful. You are not avoiding the disagreement or dancing around it.

Note that my word choice is "agree" rather than "disagree." Recall our discussion from Chapter 5 on how words create reality. In labeling it as "agree" rather than "disagree," a reality of agreement is created through our vocabulary choices, keeping the compass pointed in the direction toward which we wish to move. The focus remains on agreement rather than disagreement. And, the temporality of the situation is acknowledged. Right now and in the present tense. We do not agree *right now*. That leaves the possibility of agreeing at some point in the future.

Second, identify any factors in the situation that might change over time. Your point of view might change, their point of view might change, or the environment (the budget, the economy, the political climate, the actual climate, etc.) may change. When you acknowledge the opportunity for growth or change, including your own viewpoint, you build agreement with the other person that it may be possible to reach agreement in the future.

Third, suggest a realistic point in the future that would be an appropriate interval to revisit the issue. Depending on the issue, it might be in two days, in two weeks, in six months, or two years. Then, put that possibility into an existent system, most likely a calendar. If you agree to talk about it in two days, send a meeting invitation for two days from now. There's nothing like a placeholder on the calendar to keep an issue alive. If your interval is longer, much longer, like two years, then I suggest you put the calendar notice in your own calendar and send the meeting notice closer the time you agreed on. Unless of course, you are able to be lighthearted and not take yourself too seriously (and your colleague can do the same). Then, by all means, send the meeting notice through for two years from now!

To recap, the process has three steps:

1. Acknowledge the lack of agreement in the present tense.
2. Identify factors that might change over time.
3. Request to revisit the issue at a realistic point in the future.

When we put all three parts together it sounds like this: "Kimberly, I know we don't agree on this right now. Perhaps over time something will change. My view of the situation might change. Your view of the situation might change. Or our customer data trends might change, making it clear to both of us which way to go on this issue. I'd like to put a meeting on the calendar for us to discuss this again after our third quarter customer data reports are in. How does that sound?"

Kimberly will most likely say "yes" to this request and then, shazam, you've ended on agreement!

ACCEPT THE AGREEMENT

Even if you didn't get everything you wanted, accept the agreement. Pretending to accept the outcome when you do not is both passive-aggressive and damaging to the relationship. Sometimes we think we are "taking one for the team" when we agree to something we really don't believe in or fully agree with. The line of thinking goes something like this: "Most everyone else agrees, and I don't want to make waves/slow the process down/sit through another meeting on this topic." So feigned agreement passes as agreement. This is bald faced passive-aggressive behavior.

How do you tell the difference in whether you are pulling a passive-aggressive maneuver or if it really doesn't matter? Well, if it isn't a big deal, you won't give it much thought. The outcome may not be your preferred outcome, but you don't really give a darn. That's not passive-aggressive. It just doesn't matter much to you. And that's okay.

On the other hand, if you can't let go of it and talk about it to anyone who will listen and ruminate about it, then it was passive-aggressive to feign agreement. You'll know because you'll still be talking about it in the parking lot, the elevator, and the restroom. You won't be able to let it go. You'll be complaining and moaning that it is unfair or inappropriate or just plain wrong. Clearly, there was something to say and you didn't say it. It doesn't go away on its own. And you didn't speak up. Something is yet to be said, which is why it continues to come up, whether in your "out loud" conversations or in the privacy of your own ruminations. Never fear. There's still time. You can go back to that person or situation and remedy the issue by telling them now that you didn't agree then and ask to reopen the discussion. Use the Fact AND model to tee up the conversation as discussed in Chapter 5.

THE MEETING AFTER THE MEETING

If you are privy to conversations that demonstrate lack of agreement when there was an opportunity to voice concerns, put an end to them. For example, let's say you and your colleagues listened while the vacation policy change was announced and you all sat quietly without asking the tough questions that were on everyone's mind. Then, at the end of the day you find yourself in the parking lot amidst several of your colleagues, complaining and moaning about the new vacation policy.

This is what I call "the meeting after the meeting" and it is not good for you or your organization. When you complain and essentially "relive" the stressful situation, levels of stress hormones such as cortisol rise, which can give way to physical problems like high blood pressure and weight gain. It also brings about a sense of sadness and disempowerment ("I don't have a voice and I will never get a chance to speak up") that can damage your mental health.

If you find yourself included in "the meeting after the meeting," suggest to your colleagues that you take some productive action regarding the situation instead of just rehashing it. It might sound like this: "Yeah, none of us said anything to Susan in the meeting. Let's see if she's available first thing in the morning so that we can let her know we have some concerns."

Sometimes it isn't feasible to bring a quick end to the meeting after the meeting due to rank or organizational politics. You may feel outranked in position, years of service, or any number of other factors. If that is the case, excuse yourself from the conversation. If you remain, even if you are not an active participant in the conversation, you are guilty by association. And, there's a good chance the complainers will think you agree with them. Silence equals consent.

Recall Anthony and Eric from the beginning of the chapter. They did not reach agreement in their first conversation. They did not share the same views on whether or not developers should communicate directly with clients. It became clear to Anthony that this would be a Type 2 situation.

After some coaching on the Fact AND model so that he could tee up the next conversation without defensiveness, Anthony began by stating a premise that both he and Eric shared. "Making our customers happy and keeping them happy is critical in our business," he began. Eric nodded. Anthony continued, "We don't agree right now on how to best make that happen." Eric nodded again. "How about we both do some research with our teams about how to best handle direct client communication and then talk again in a few days?" Eric consented.

Agreement, even inside of disagreement, is possible.

CONCLUSION

As you work on creating agreement, use the exercises at the end of the chapter to strategize agreement and keep yourself accountable.

Presumably, you've cleared your emotional state, opened the conversation without making the other person defensive, practiced good listening skills and asked questions using objective inquiry, acknowledged the various stories that are at play in the situation and now, have reached some sort of agreement (or are actively working toward agreement with a series of small agreements if it is a Type 2 situation).

Great work! You are on your way to a life that is more courageous, direct, and intentional, one in which you can take the tough stuff life throws at you *head on*.

EXERCISES

#15: Accept the Agreement

Sometimes we don't get everything we want in an agreement. This is especially true when we weren't the one to initiate the difficult conversation. When that is the case, it is important to give voice to our concerns as we work toward agreement and then be accepting of the agreement for now. We can always reopen the issue at a later date, but for now we need to accept it.

Jot down a few situations from the past where you have agreed on the surface, but not fully accepted the agreement or solution.

Now think about the durability of those agreements. Did they hold, even though you were not 100% on board? If the agreement fell apart, how did it fail? Did you negotiate a new agreement?

#16: Agreeing Inside of Disagreement

There is a way to acknowledge a lack of agreement and leave room for a different outcome. I call it "agreeing inside of disagreement" and there are three parts to the process.

1. First, clearly and straightforwardly acknowledge the lack of agreement in the present tense. For example, "We do not agree on an outcome for this situation right now."

2. Identify any factors in the situation that might change over time. Your point of view, their point of view, or environmental factors may change.

3. Suggest a realistic point in the future that would make sense to revisit the issue and put that date on the calendar.

Think of a situation where you currently don't have agreement. Write out what it would sound like to have the "agreeing inside of disagreement" conversation.

Part 3

Difficult Conversations in Context

CHAPTER 9

Tackling Tough Stuff in Teams and Meetings

"Let me back up to give a little more context on this," James interjected into the meeting. As he began to share two decades worth of history, Elizabeth felt like she could recite it along with him. She struggled to contain her frustration. Her chest tightened, she felt her eyes widen and she balled her fists in her lap. After a couple of sentences she burst out, "James, we all know the history of the agency. You don't have to begin in the 1960s every time you have an idea. Get to the point. What is it?"

James recoiled physically as if he'd been slapped. Others shifted uncomfortably in their seats. Although James rambled on about the past frequently during meetings, he usually concluded his remarks with a contribution that helped the team. This time, he wasn't given the chance to get there.

James stammered for a moment and then said, "I've lost my train of thought." He looked at his notebook, uncomfortable and unable to make eye contact with his colleagues. He'd never been dressed down like that in a meeting in his two and half decades with the company. The meeting continued with James unable to find his voice. He was humiliated. And furious. Serious damage was done to the relationship between James and Elizabeth.

Competing agendas, difficult personalities, and office politics often give rise to difficult conversations in team settings and in meetings. This chapter discusses team and meeting dynamics and offers exercises and techniques to use in those contexts to turn difficult conversations into creative, constructive conversations and promote healthy, productive disagreement without doing damage to individual or team relationships.

Team members, by their very nature, bring a diverse set of skills and talents to their group: the whole becomes greater than the sum of its parts. The diversity in a well-constructed team, be it diversity of race, ethnicity, gender, religion, or diversity of thought, will inevitably lend itself to disagreement and competing points of view. When handled effectively, creative disagreement contributes to higher-quality outcomes. When handled ineffectively, competing points of view can lead to disengagement, hurt feelings, and lower output, as we saw with James' reaction to Elizabeth's outburst.

Whether in a team setting or in a meeting, difficult conversations may stem from differences in approach to the work itself or they may originate from personality and communication style differences that impede collaboration. Regardless of the source, the dynamic of holding a difficult conversation becomes more complex in teams and meetings because more people are typically in attendance and involved. It is no longer a conversation between a duo as described in earlier chapters.

We will look at a variety of difficult and dysfunctional phenomena that occur in meetings and teams. First, we look at conflicts that stem from interruptions and we examine the importance of equal turns in meetings. Then we turn our attention to sabotage or "being thrown under the bus." Finally, we look at conflict and how to channel such conflict into productive conflict where new and better ideas can emerge.

INTERRUPTIONS

One rainy Sunday, when I was eight years old, I recall sitting with my parents and two older brothers around the dinner table. Everyone had something to share, we were all highly animated, and we were all talking over each other in bursts and shouts. Not a single one of us was discussing the same topic. Several minutes into the chaos, there was a brief pause. I couldn't take it any longer, and found myself declaring (in my most grown-up voice), "This is NOT a conversation—we have to take turns!"

As an adult, I now understand just how crucial turn-taking is to the success of any group endeavor—especially at work. For example, research published in the journal *Science* found that groups whose members foster equal individual participation—both in terms of numbers of turns and length of turns—consistently demonstrate higher quality decision-making skills and an increase in overall group performance results.[22]

Researchers from Carnegie Mellon, MIT and Union College were curious to know if there was a "collective" intelligence of groups that could be measured, much like we measure individual intelligence with IQ tests. They wondered if some groups were more intelligent than others, and if so, was it simply because the average IQ of the group was higher, or was there something else at play? To test their hypothesis, the researchers conducted a series of experiments. First, research participants were given two assessments, one that measured their IQ and one that measured their social sensitivity, or their ability to "read the mind in the eyes" of others. Then they were placed in small groups to perform decision-making tasks. Researchers evaluated the outcomes of the small groups' decisions to see if the groups who had the highest average IQ made the best decisions (meaning individual intelligence was the best predictor of group outcomes) or if there was a collective intelligence, meaning other factors were better predictors of outcomes.

The researchers' hypothesis was confirmed. Some groups performed better than others, even though the individual IQ scores of the participants were not as high as those in other groups. Indeed, there was such a thing as collective intelligence. The researchers found that the groups that made the best decisions had three clear characteristics in common: they included people who scored higher on the social sensitivity assessment, they were groups with more women than men,* and in the conversation, team members took more or less equal numbers of turns. Groups with these characteristics consistently outperformed the other groups on the problem-solving tasks.

Overall, the research shines a light on the role of turn-taking in effective collaboration and decision making. It demonstrates that no matter how intelligent an individual might be, it is how he or she interacts with others that brings value to a team or meeting. Says

---

*Researchers posit that women tend to be better at accurately assessing other's emotions, accounting for the unanticipated finding that more women in the group led to higher collective intelligence. In the experiments, if the group was predominantly or entirely women, the group no longer outperformed the other groups. The bottom line: gender balance is important.

lead researcher Anita Woolley, "It really calls into question our whole notion of what intelligence is. What individuals can do all by themselves is becoming less important; what matters more is what they can do with others."[23]

One of the chief obstacles to equal turn-taking is people who hijack other people's turns, or interrupt. Interruptions are one of the primary sources of conflict in the workplace. When people are interrupted, they feel disrespected. That disrespect can quickly spiral into quiet (or not so quiet) anger and disengagement. Meetings, because of the dialogue and exchange of ideas that is associated with them, are a rich breeding ground for interruptions. The sting of disrespect is more acute in a meeting as well, because with five or ten of your colleagues as an audience, the disrespect feels magnified.

Turn-taking isn't always easy. Perceptions about hierarchy, expertise, even our conditioned beliefs about gender and diversity (whether conscious or unconscious) can all contribute to roadblocks that prevent beneficial and equal collaboration in meetings. Knowing what you now know about the importance of turn-taking in effective decision making, you can begin to subtly monitor turns in the meetings you attend and make interjections to distribute turns more equally.

Overcoming Interruptions

Better outcomes begin with mindfulness. Are you the one who chronically seizes the spotlight, or do you find yourself constantly losing center stage? Are you the frequent witness of unfortunate interruptions, but don't know whether or how to intervene? Knowing that interruptions tend to lead to unequal turns in meetings, and consequently less intelligent outcomes, can provide inspiration to strive for more balanced conversations in meetings. With that awareness in mind, approach interruptions head on with the strategies outlined below.

1. To get the turn: Make direct eye contact with the person who has the turn, lean forward, and frown ever so slightly. This non-verbal cue will help signal your desire to interject or adjust the direction of the conversation, once the current speaker is done sharing.

2. To keep the turn: Resist the urge to make eye contact with people who start squirming for their turn to speak before you are finished. If that's not enough, hold up your hand in the direction of that person with your palm facing them, a gesture that means "stop," and subtly shake your head while you continue talking.

3. To regain the turn if you've been interrupted: Hold your ground and interrupt right back. Try saying something quick and clear like, "George, I wasn't finished," and continue with your thought.

4. To mitigate ongoing interruption issues: Prepare in advance with a confederate who is willing to interject on your behalf and give the turn back. For women, like it or not, it works best if your confederate is a man. A confederate intervention might sound like this: "Wait, I want to hear what Lisa was saying. Lisa?"

5. To give the turn after you've finished: Try passing the turn to someone on your team whose voice is historically underrepresented. Or, if you know there are already multiple group members waiting to respond to your ideas, call them out in order like this: "Lisa, I know you've been waiting to respond, and then George."

Next, we examine sabotage and the accompanying amygdala hijack that happens when it catches us unawares.

SABOTAGE

Julie and Daniel were collaborating on a proposal for entering a new market with one of their company's products. The big day had come; after four months of research and hard work, they were making their pitch to the senior management team. They had shared preliminary research and conclusions with their manager and various stakeholders during the previous months, seeking feedback and input along the way. They felt prepared.

Part way through their presentation, it became clear that the Chief Operating Officer was not in favor of their proposed approach. He was beginning to sway others on the management team through persuasive but empty rhetoric, circumventing the data driven argument Julie and Daniel were making.

Much to Julie's surprise, Daniel changed course and aligned himself with the COO. "That's what I've been trying to tell Julie all these months," Daniel asserted. Even though many of the ideas in the presentation that the COO was shooting down were his own, Daniel went on, agreeing with the prevailing opinion of the outspoken COO and abandoning his research partner. Julie was flabbergasted. She'd been thrown under the bus before, but never to this degree. Julie grappled with feeling blindsided and with the enormity of the situation, struggling to find her voice. What would it take to professionally disagree with the senior management team and the COO without her colleague's support? And further, how could she show the management team that the ideas being presented were just as much Daniel's ideas as they were hers?

Intentional sabotage and becoming a victim of office politics are not uncommon occurrences in the workplace. Think about the last time you were caught unawares by a colleague in a meeting. Perhaps you assumed the two of you agreed on the topic and instead your colleague cut your opinion down, humiliating you in the process. Were you able to speak up in the moment and advocate for yourself? Or were you rendered speechless as Julie was, struck dumb in the midst of being caught off-guard? Your reaction may vary, especially as the stakes and the people involved differ. In Julie's case, the stakes were quite high and the audience included the most senior leaders in the organization.

In situations like these, the prefrontal cortex is likely to go offline as adrenaline, cortisol, and other stress hormones are released, mobilizing the body for defense. The R-brain is engaged and is preparing to defend the sense of self that feels attacked. It is more important than ever to remain present and fully engaged, calm and centered, in order to sort out the situation and correct any misinterpretations or allegations as they occur, or as soon thereafter as possible. While it may be tempting to throw the other person under the proverbial bus, it is critical to handle the situation professionally and assertively.

Approaching Sabotage

Julie is essentially experiencing an amygdala hijack and as such she has three possible innate responses: fight, flight, or freeze. As you learned in earlier chapters, one of these responses will kick in unless deliberate and conscious action is taken. That is the nature of the human body, working on a stimulus-response basis. In a full-on fight or flight response, as you will recall from Chapter 3, the neo-cortex will go offline and Julie's complex language skills, abstract thinking, imagination, and curiosity will become inaccessible.

If Julie goes down the path of fight, she will become antagonistic and aggressive with Daniel during the presentation. That attitude will most likely spill over and influence the way she addresses the management team in the meeting, particularly the COO. A response fueled by rage and anger will come across as unprofessional to the senior management team members and may put Julie's job and career advancement opportunities in jeopardy.

If Julie freezes and does not respond, she will yield control of the meeting and its direction to the COO and Daniel. She will take a backseat to Daniel and his approach through the rest of the presentation and fail to advocate for her position. If she remains frozen, her shock will prevent her from participating in the meeting in a meaningful way. She may find herself wishing she could say something but feeling essentially immobilized.

If Julie takes flight (even if she stays in the room), she will cow to Daniel's position. She will mentally "check out" of the meeting and will feel much like she is watching the episode unfold from a distance. Much like the freeze response, Julie's participation will drop off considerably. She may be acutely aware of what is being said, but feel like she is not an active player in the conversation, as if she is watching the meeting on television.

While one of these responses is likely to be Julie's initial, unfiltered response, none of them are effective for her. Further, none of these responses will serve Julie's career or the company's best interests. Let's walk through what it would look like if Julie were to take a head-on approach.

First, Julie will need to put some space between the stimulus and her response. To find that space, she might anchor to a physical object on her body like her glasses or her wedding band as described in Chapter 4. As she anchors, she can acknowledge the response she is having ("I'm angry with Daniel and I can't believe he's throwing me under the bus!") and then consciously choose how she'd like to carry on. Julie's self-talk might sound something like this: "I'm going to use the Fact AND approach to bring this discussion to a close and I'm going to try to remain as neutral as possible while I do that. I am Switzerland."

After anchoring, Julie must make a deliberate choice about her next move: she will need to take the situation head on and be assertive. Julie's response might sound something like this: "Allow me to recap our discussion so far. Daniel and I presented data and a recommended direction. Other opinions and suggestions were added to the discussion. I know many of you felt differently about the proposed direction before the meeting than you do now. The new ideas put forth by Craig (the COO) are indeed compelling. I propose that Daniel and I take those ideas back for additional research before we move ahead with a decision. I know how important it is to all of you and to our shareholders that we make data-driven decisions." Julie may have to assert this position several times to shift the momentum of the meeting.

Note that Julie doesn't specifically address Daniel or his changing allegiance in her assertive stance. She may be tempted to dress Daniel down to make him feel as she felt (there's that human tendency to reciprocate again!). However, that does not serve the outcome she is after. Rather, she can best speak with Daniel about his shift in perspective and the consequences it had for her and their professional relationship in a private conversation, again using a head-on approach. It is likely in a situation like this that it will take two or more conversations with Daniel to reach agreement. Julie would be wise to follow the steps for a Type 2 agreement outlined in Chapter 8 as she proceeds.

Next, we turn to transforming an antagonizing conflict into one that has an opportunity to give way to original, innovative solutions that would not otherwise have come about.

CREATIVE CONFLICT

As they prepared for their next product launch, Jerry and Tanya arrived at a major hiccup in the creative process. Advertising campaign proofs had just come in and the tone of the key message and the visuals were both off the mark. With only a short window of time until the campaign launch, tensions were high.

Jerry was convinced that the solution was to fire the outside ad agency and start over. Tanya felt that their in-house marketing team could salvage the expensive work from the external agency and get the campaign back on track. Neither could move beyond their own fixed way of thinking.

They went to others on their team. The prevailing opinion among other team members was that the campaign was fine and could run as delivered from the agency. Tanya and Jerry had more accountability for this project than others on the team. The two of them were further infuriated by the dissenters who thought the campaign was "fine." According to Tanya, Jerry was being inflexible and aloof. Jerry thought Tanya was overly optimistic and naïve. After discussing the problem on multiple occasions, the conflict was starting to seem insurmountable.

What is happening with Jerry and Tanya and how can they get through it? Whether it is a larger group or the dynamic of a pair within a larger team setting like Tanya and Jerry, internal conflict often leads team members to become defensive. When they are defensive, they are unable to hear one another's ideas, so much so that they don't interpret their colleagues' contributions as they were intended. This is a common result of defensiveness. As psychological defenses go up, listening ability declines. In the case of a team, other people and processes are involved. For the sake of the issue at hand and for the overall health and well-being of the team, it is important to reach agreement amicably and resolutely.

For Jerry and Tanya to find resolution, they are going to have to give up their fixed thinking. They face an excellent opportunity to shift gears and walk into what I refer to as creative conflict. To embrace creative conflict, you must make a choice to consciously let go of "my way" versus "your way" thinking and transcend face-value differences. If you implement what you learned in Part 2 of this book, working hard to listen to one another and remain curious about the other person's position, you can capitalize on the conflict and allow more creative solutions to emerge. You will need to honor points of disagreement and not take those points of disagreement personally, while also making room for new and inspired solutions. Using creative conflict as an ultimate form of collaboration, Jerry and Tanya can reach a better outcome than either could have arrived at on their own.

One or both will need to shift into a place of curiosity about the other's position. Once there, they will need to ask more questions and listen deeply to the answers. Suspending the view that your own answer is the right or best answer is tricky business. Often, we are so committed to our position that the commitment becomes a hindrance to good decision making. For either Jerry or Tanya to shift their position so they can be in creative conflict, they will need to step away from the situation for a moment.

Oftentimes physical distance helps create the emotional distance needed to address a situation head on. Taking a short walk, even if only to the restroom or coffee station, can help create that distance. With newfound emotional distance, imagine at least three different ways the problem might be addressed. For Jerry that might include Tanya's way of thinking, taking seriously his colleagues' sentiment that the campaign really is adequate as is, and reaching out to a colleague at another agency to see if they could put together a creative solution quickly.

Next, Jerry could go back to Tanya with his newfound commitment to solving the problem and share his ideas and be open to her response. To be in creative conflict, he will look to find some points of agreement with something she says, even if they are minor points of convergence at first. It is critical at this point that they share agreement on something, even if it is merely the acknowledgement that they are in a challenging situation. From this place, it is much more likely that the two of them will be able to work through the conflict to find a creative solution—one that will be built upon the best ideas they both have to offer. The steps for transforming an antagonistic conflict into a creative conflict are outlined below.

Moving from Conflict to Collaboration

Turning a disagreement into a creative conflict uses elements of the Fact AND method, as well as some of the skills we discussed in Chapter 7 regarding considering other viewpoints, and how to disagree with possibility.

The next time you find yourself in a conflict, follow the steps below to turn it into a creative conflict:

1. Take a walk to recharge. Create some healthy distance between yourself and the conflict if things start to feel sticky. The best option is to get outside. The

most important thing is that you give your mind time to wander and open.

2. After recharging, challenge yourself to find three fresh perspectives. That's right, three. What position does your colleague hold? What impact does the conflict have on your team, customers, and key stakeholders? What outcome would be best for the organization as a whole? Force yourself to see the bigger picture.

3. Re-enter the situation and work to agree with your colleague on a definition of the problem. Conflicts stem from a simple misunderstanding more often than you'd think.

4. Find something to agree on. If you disagree on exactly what to do about the defined problem, find something more general that you can agree on and then work on the bigger issue from there—I call this "notching it up a level."

5. Say out loud—to your colleague(s)—what you think they want, and why. Use the following framework: "If I believed that [insert what your colleague wants], I'd probably be thinking that [insert any theory that would support the colleague's premise]." Your theory will probably be wrong and your colleague will need to correct you. That's the point of the exercise! Take turns repeating this process to encourage clarity and understanding.

6. Allow the conflict to naturally morph into creative discussion. You are now more open to solutions and engaging in greater collaboration. Pat yourself on the back—you've earned it.

CONCLUSION

In this chapter, we've examined three of the most common situations that give rise to difficult conversations in teams and meetings: interruptions, sabotage, and conflict. Use the exercises at the end of this chapter to strengthen the skills we have considered for improving discussions within workgroups. In the next chapter, we turn our attention to the challenging discussions that come with shared spaces.

EXERCISES

#17: Finding Common Ground

One of the fastest ways to turn the tide on a conflict with a colleague is to find common ground. Find something you can agree on. You might want to start with coming to agreement on exactly what the problem is or what factors are causing the problem. Alternatively, you can look to adjacent spaces to find an area of agreement (i.e., the schedule on this project feels practically impossible). From there, notch it up a level by talking about other areas of the project or situation where you have common ground. Acknowledge that there are parts of the situation you agree on. From here, it will be easier to notch it up again and get closer to the source of the problem and a new solution.

Think of a situation where you and a colleague had a clash in your approaches to a challenge. Write down the different points of view and then make suggestions for how each party can see the other's side.

#18: Be a Turn Researcher

The next time you attend a recurring meeting (e.g., weekly) with the same attendees, subtly keep track of how many turns and of what length (relatively speaking) each team member takes. How close is the group to having equal turns, both in numbers and in length?

If you find the turns are not equal, use some of the strategies outlined earlier in this chapter to influence a more equal turn distribution.

Use this space to note how much each person talks during your meeting. You may also use it to note who interrupts others and who shies away from participating.

CHAPTER 10

Challenges in Cubicles, Cafeterias, and Common Areas

Ryan rounded the corner on the way to his office and caught a glimpse of the copy machine. A handwritten sign with the words "Fix Me" scrawled in a Sharpie was taped to the front of it. Ryan's emotions surged. He wasn't sure which he was more upset about: that the copier was out of order again or the passive-aggressive behavior from whichever colleague put the sign on it.

A project manager at a large retail organization, Ryan had been working with his team on being more straightforward and open in their communication. It was a grassroots effort. As a project manager, he didn't have a budget or approval to bring in any outside help such as a consultant or a trainer, but he was bound and determined to turn the tide of the passive-aggressive behavior of the employees on the project he was overseeing.

It hadn't been easy going. Many of the people on the project didn't think their behavior was passive-aggressive. So when Ryan tried to have an open dialogue with them about communicating differently, without passive-aggressive overtones, they got defensive.

"I'm NOT passive-aggressive," Gwen had responded. "I just soften the blow when I deliver bad news," she posited. In more than one team meeting, Gwen made comments directed toward Ryan that sounded incredibly passive-aggressive to him. "Ryan, I was surprised to see that the deadlines for Phase 2 have moved," she remarked in a meeting the other day. Ryan had briefed her on those exact changes several hours before the meeting. Why was she feigning surprise in front of the entire team?

When Ryan spoke to her about it later, she replied, "I was sure others had the same question, so I was really speaking on their behalf. I was doing you a favor."

Really? It didn't feel like a favor to Ryan. He'd shared the new dates with her in advance, expecting her support in the meeting. This felt like backstabbing.

Ryan swung by the copier and removed the sign. He circled over to the other side of the hallway where the administrative assistant sat and he asked her to call the service team. Again. Then he went back to his desk to strategize one more time about how to address the passive-aggressive behavior in his project team.

If you are like most people, you are probably not actively seeking out difficult situations or conversations—instead, these challenging moments find *you*. Frustrations plague us every day, from the co-worker who steals your food from the breakroom refrigerator to the person who spills in the cafeteria and runs, to the passive-aggressive pest who jams the photocopier and merely leaves behind a sign that says "fix me" like Ryan experienced. With the trend of open floorplans and agile work environments, such situations are becoming more and more common.

These examples, while relatively minor, can still be incredibly disruptive for the culprit's co-workers or any others who share the same space. In these situations, a disproportionate amount of energy is often spent on frustration, anger, lack of productivity, and gossip. Without effective tools for constructing conversations, sensitive issues tend to be deferred . . . and sometimes, when these relatively mundane situations begin to drive you insane, you might snap and say something without the diplomacy and tact you wished you'd used. Outcomes from situations like these range from frustrating conversations in which feelings are hurt and miscommunication occurs to the involvement of a manager or human resources. To reach resolution and keep these situations from becoming a drag on resources, it is necessary to approach them head on, and with the perfect mix of directness and grace. This chapter provides tools to do just that, and prevent the small but intrusive annoyances of shared spaces from becoming big problems.

WE'RE ALL IN THIS TOGETHER: SHARED SPACES

Martin loved his new FitBit. And everyone in the office knew it. Co-workers adored Martin. He was friendly and outgoing and a dependable colleague. And in the past 12 months, Martin lost over 50 pounds and became very focused on his health. He had another 30 pounds to go to reach his goal weight and he was very motivated. The whole office was incredibly proud of him. And then he got a FitBit and began tracking his steps.

In his role as an account manager, he spent most of his workday on conference calls with clients and colleagues in other locations. Once he began wearing his FitBit, he became obsessed with getting as many steps in each day as he possibly could. He began taking his conference calls on his headset while walking around. If his work area had been all offices with closed doors, that might have been fine. But Martin worked in a sea of cubicles. As he walked up and down the cubicle hallways on his conference calls, he talked. Loudly. Coworkers were distracted as they tried to focus on their own work, amidst the sound of Martin's roving voice.

You've probably faced a situation like this. Whether it is a FitBit walker-talker, someone using a speakerphone in an open office plan, or someone discussing the details of their personal life in areas where you could clearly overhear them despite not wanting to, you have felt the disruption and wanted to say something. And perhaps you did. But for many people, situations like these are awkward because they span both personal and professional boundaries. If you've ever been told, "If you don't have something nice to say, don't say anything at all," you may feel uncomfortable raising these sorts of topics. Let's look at some common reactions to this situation and then provide guidance about how to approach issues like these head on.

Venting

When frustration mounts at work, you may feel inclined to "vent" about it to another co-worker. While venting is often thought of as a harmless coping mechanism, it can actually do more harm than good. An assumption that goes back at least to the work of Sigmund Freud is that expression of emotion will help to dissipate that emotion. The prevailing hypothesis of Freud's time was that emotion was energy and if it remained trapped in someone's body it could lead to psychosomatic, or stress-based illness. The sentiment was that venting, or airing the troubling matter, would lead to catharsis and the person would be freed from the troubling emotions.

Unfortunately, this is not an accurate theory about how human emotions function. Studies during the past few decades have demonstrated quite the opposite. Whether talking aloud to someone or simply ruminating silently about it, the outcomes are the same: it does more harm than good. As psychologist Jill Littrell notes, venting makes matters worse.[24] In one set of experiments, participants were divided into two groups. Individuals in both groups were provoked to be angry. Half of the participants vented their feelings of anger and irritation and the other half were distracted by the researchers with a different task rather than being allowed to vent. The participants who vented were shown to be *more* bothered by the thing that provoked them, even after time had passed. The other group, the ones who were given a distraction by the researchers instead of venting, were significantly less bothered after the same amount of time passed.

Venting is in fact, a poor substitute for confronting the problem and taking appropriate action. Why is this so? In the moment, as you are venting about the problem, your brain responds with some of the same regions that are responsible for problem-solving. Because talking about it partially relieves your distress, you are less inclined to take action toward remedying the situation. Your brain, to a certain extent, acts as if you've solved the problem.

Researcher Jeffrey Lohr demonstrated that anger will dissipate faster if you try to control it than if you vent it.[25] He and his research colleagues found that discussing the anger magnified it, whereas consciously and deliberately controlling it (distracting was one of the techniques used to control it), lessened the anger. However, it is worth noting that Lohr found a significant difference between venting about anger versus sadness. When sharing your feelings about sadness or depression, those emotions get validated and your pain begins to lessen, making it a good technique for somber or bleak situations. Anger on the other hand, is strengthened and intensified through venting.

As you review your anger or frustration with another person by discussing it out loud, you are actually reinforcing it, making it stronger, and giving it more power. Your neuropathways are getting stronger and stronger, bolstering the memory and increasing the likelihood that this situation will continue to replay in your brain. Neuroscientists use the phrase "synapses that fire together wire together." When you have a thought, brain synapses, or small connections in the brain, are set off and make connections across spaces where previously there were none, essentially adding new neuropathways, or wiring, to your brain. The more often the thought is repeated, the stronger the pathway becomes.

That new pattern is also likely to make you more upset the next time a similar event occurs. The neuropathways are already there and your response becomes easier and easier to produce. We have the prefrontal cortex to thank for this. It not only allows us to simulate the future by having an experience in our minds before we try it out in real life as discussed in Chapter 3, we can also replay experiences we've had in the past.

Will This Help or Harm the Relationship?

If you are continually venting to the same person, you may also be doing harm to the relationship. Imagine a person who comes to you on a near daily basis to complain. How likely are you to give a warm welcome to that person and positively anticipate their arrival? Regularly sharing your troubling emotions with a colleague at work (or a friend or family member outside of work, for that matter) can corrode the relationship. You might think of it as emotional littering.

However, the complaining may land differently depending on how well you know each other and the context of your relationship. Other studies have found that in close relationships, co-rumination, or replaying negative situations with one another, makes people feel more attached to each another. The tone and attitude with which you share those negative situations makes a big difference, too. When the talk is focused on preventing the situation from occurring again and making you feel like you have agency in the matter, according to Margot Bastin, a researcher at the University of Leuven in Belgium,[26] it is referred to as "co-reflection" and is a positive and constructive technique. If the sharing addresses the problem in a passive way however, expressing anger and disappointment while focusing on the bad consequences and predicting further catastrophe, it is known as "co-brooding". Co-brooding is likely to do more harm than good, regardless of whether it is a close relationship or not.

Approaching Shared Space Conversations

What should one do, rather than ruminate or complain to others? Approach the situation head on, of course. Let's start with how you might use the head on approach with Martin, the walking, talking FitBit fitness fanatic:

"Martin, I know your health is extremely important to you and you must be very proud of the progress you've made in taking better care of your body. Your FitBit is a new addition to the mix . . . and as you take your "walk and talk" meetings, you come by my desk frequently talking rather loudly. It's distracting to me and is interfering with my work. Can we schedule some time to talk about it and come up with another solution that works for both of us?"

THE OFFICE KITCHEN AREA

I was recently guest lecturing a university class on the topic of how to have difficult conversations and sharing the method I've described in this book. I selected an example that I thought students could relate to: roommates not taking care of their own dishes (leaving them in the sink, common areas, etc.). They agreed; it was a problem that many of them experienced. When I began to give examples of similar situations, both at home and at the office, one young man, looking exasperated, raised his hand and said, "Dr. Anderson, do you mean to say that even long after I've graduated and moved on from college, I'm still going to have to deal with the issue of dirty dishes?" Indeed, young man, dishes will continue to haunt you if you allow them to. Better to learn how to address them head on earlier in life rather than later.

Not cleaning up shared spaces at work (and at home) is a perennial issue. *Why* people don't clean up after themselves is a topic for a different expert. I don't make any claims about people's motivation or lack thereof. Rather, I offer an approach for discussing it with them directly to remedy the situation. Whether it is dishes in the sink in a common area at work, spoiled items left in a communal refrigerator, failing to start the next pot of coffee when you've just taken the last cup, or spilling in the cafeteria and not cleaning it up, the issue of food and dishes is one that is not likely to go away as long as we humans still need to eat.

You might initially try to take the high road, thinking you can transcend this pesky little issue. Pick your battles and all that. And yet, day after day, coffee cup after coffee cup, it piles up. And eats away at you. I'm here to tell you that if you don't approach it head on, and fairly soon after you begin to take notice, it will become a much larger issue in your mind than it may be in real life. Better for everyone involved then, for you to address it while it is still small potatoes. Let's look at an example of how to approach a situation like this head on.

Approaching Kitchen Cleanup

In this case, I'm going to take a "let's solve this together" approach. When you are working on an issue that occurs in a communal area, there is a great deal of room to pass the buck and avoid responsibility. If you come on too strong in a situation like this, it can look like you are stalking the person or the kitchen area, trying to "catch" the person in the act. That creates a culture of suspicion and mistrust. Of course, if you work in a very small office and there is no possibility of the culprit being someone else, then I would use the more direct approach modeled throughout the rest of this book. However, presuming there are many people who share the kitchen area, I suggest an approach like the one modeled below.

"Scott, I know you love your coffee as much as the next person ... probably even more so. Three times in the past two weeks I've come to get a cup of joe and the pot's been left empty. Now I know you're not the only one who leaves it empty. I'm hoping we can come up with a plan so that it doesn't happen anymore. Can I count on you to help?"

Scott may counter with excuses and attempt to avoid responsibility. Be ready for this and if it happens, stand ready to be more firm. If his response is, "I know, but I was so busy this morning. I was going to stop back later to do it and when I did, there was already a fresh pot." Then, you say something like this: "Hey, I know, we are all busy. And I want you to know that this isn't personal to you. The same goes for everyone. If you and I have some variation of this conversation with everyone who uses the area, I know we will see lasting impact. And that means there will always be a piping hot cup of coffee for both of us when we want it. How about it, are you on board?"

In this follow up, the focus is on not making Scott feel singled out. After first giving a nod to his excuse/s (i.e., too busy), move into an approach that says this is a communal issue. We accomplish this two ways. First, we specifically say that it isn't personal. Then, throughout the remainder of your turn in the conversation, use plenty of plural pronouns. We. Us. Everyone. In doing so, you are taking the focus off of Scott and putting it on the community who shares the area. (Note: If you know Scott is a repeat offender and one of the main sources of the problem, this is not the right approach and would be one that I deem passive-aggressive.)

Someone like Scott might not take to the change and immediately implement new behaviors. I encourage you to be persistent. Continue to address the issue with him over time until his behavior changes, always keeping the focus on the community at large, with the use of plural pronouns. Perhaps Scott has not had the responsibility for refilling the coffee pot in his personal life. If so, the change in behavior make take some time to bring about. Keep in mind, too, that the changed behavior you are striving for is for the good of the community, and while it may have some personal benefit for you, it also benefits others across the organization. Of course, be mindful to not become a nag or to only have conversations with Scott about the coffee! Strike up a collegial relationship with him if you don't have one already or if you don't work together directly. Inquire about his family, hobbies and weekends. Be likable. People do favors for those whom they like.

PERSONAL HYGIENE AND OTHER FAUX PAS

The number of social blunders and indiscretions clients and audience members share with me, especially those related to personal hygiene, never ceases to amaze me. Americans spend a great deal of time at work (upwards of 47 hours per week according to a recent study)[27] and clearly some of them are very comfortable there, as comfortable as if they were in their own home. From clipping toenails at their desk to passionately kissing a coworker at the office to spending time on questionable websites (for organizations who don't have those blocked), some employees lack discernment regarding acceptable behavior in the workplace.

Enter you. You get to be the fortunate one to share with them the norms of professional behavior in the workplace. Of course, with the tools from this book, you can do so in a manner that will have them thanking you.

Before we get into the specifics about what to say, let me add that this technique will also work for the colleague who is loudly munching their food when you need quiet, wearing strong perfume that disturbs your concentration, using no personal hygiene products and reeking of body odor, or suffering from chronic halitosis (and unintentionally making those around him suffer, too). Okay, now let's get to it.

Approaching Personal Hygiene

First, if this is really bothering you, or if you think you might lose your pluck and avoid the conversation altogether, I recommend using the Phone-A-Friend technique. Make sure someone knows you are going to have the conversation. It will give you a chance to clear any emotional issues that might get in the way, particularly if the situation, issue, or person disgusts you. It will also give you an opportunity to hold yourself accountable to have the conversation and you might possibly use the call to rehearse what you are going to say. It is critically important, though, that if you are using the Phone-A-Friend technique, you have complete and total integrity about it. This is not a chance to gossip or complain about the person or the situation. It is merely a technique for setting aside your charged emotions so you can come to the conversation with your message and your intended outcome clearly in focus. Once you are clear, you are ready to hold the conversation.

In most situations, and throughout the earlier chapters in this book, I recommend starting with a fact or a strongly held belief or opinion that you both share. In this case, I'm going to suggest something a bit different. I suggest that as you begin you acknowledge that this is an awkward or difficult conversation. I refer to this as using a sensitivity cue. Sensitivity cues foreshadow that the topic about to be raised may be perceived as delicate, discreet, or distressing to some. Examples of sensitivity cues include "This is an uncomfortable topic," "I'm not sure how to put this delicately," or "I'm a bit embarrassed to bring this up."

Using a sensitivity cue does two things. First, it creates a more equal playing field. You are about to put the other person in a vulnerable position by discussing a matter that is personal to them (i.e., hygiene). In stating that you are uncomfortable, you have already acknowledged your own vulnerability, making it easier for them to be vulnerable too. Second, it gives them a moment to orient to the idea that this conversation is different in nature than those that address typical work tasks. As with any difficult conversation, hold this one out of earshot of others in your organization.

The conversation might begin with a sensitivity cue followed by the Fact AND model you learned in Chapter 5, such as: "Hey Jim, can we talk for a few minutes? I need to talk to you as my colleague and my friend, and this an uncomfortable topic for me. And it's an important topic. Please bear with me if I'm awkward as I say this. It's about clipping toenails at work. I understand that hygiene matters like clipping toe nails are, well, personal. And it's something I'd prefer you kept in your personal space at home, not here at the office."

Expect that the person might be embarrassed and don't belabor the point. It's also best if you keep the conversation about just this topic and not "sandwich" the issue between other more palatable issues (see Chapter 5 for details). Keep the conversation short and to the point, without being rude or abrupt. Allow them space to save face if they are embarrassed. However, if the person disagrees with you and claims the behavior is perfectly acceptable, this may become a situation requiring Type 2 agreement, where it takes two or more conversations to reach agreement (see Chapter 8).

PASSIVE-AGGRESSIVE COLLEAGUES

Matthew recently joined the marketing team at a large consumer products company. He had taken a lateral move from the sales organization. Dana, one of the other members of the team, was a veteran of the team and liked to be helpful, especially with newcomers as they found their groove on the team. Their manager had encouraged Dana to mentor Matthew as he came up to speed, much as she had done with other new marketing team members. Matthew had a college degree in business with a concentration in marketing but had not worked directly in the marketing field until now. Consequently, Dana didn't always know when Matthew needed extra guidance or the extent to which he needed it. Dana often tried a soft approach, such as "Not sure if you've done a creative brief for the photography team before, but you'll want to make sure you include a complete list of the shots you want them to get, including the most minor details, like the angle of the lighting on the product and the model's face."

"Yup," Matthew responded, as he often did. The "yup" infuriated Dana. It wasn't so much the word itself but rather the tone in which he uttered it. Dana interpreted that one little syllable as meaning that Matthew thought he knew everything and he didn't need her guidance, and that further, he was annoyed that she would even consider providing any assistance. And that she even existed.

To make matters worse, every time Dana heard Matthew's "Yup," she also heard her husband's voice. It was the same reaction she got from him frequently. Recently, she had mentioned to her husband that their daughter might need some extra help with math and that they should consider hiring a tutor for her. What she was hoping would turn into a meaningful discussion about their daughter's academic progress, instead was cut short with his, "Yup." In that "yup," Dana heard "it's obvious that she needs a tutor; that's been my idea all along and you don't need to talk about it, in fact, why haven't you hired a tutor yet?" Dana is projecting her own meaning of the "yup," thinking both her husband and her colleague are being passive-aggressive. At this point she is guessing and she may or may not be accurate.

We need to know the meaning behind the "yup" or any other communication we deem passive-aggressive. We must have an accurate sense of the meaning of what is being said to determine whether there is an aggressive intent or if we are making up meaning that doesn't ring true for the other person (as we humans often do). Next we address how to do just that.

Approaching Passive-Aggressive Behavior

In this case, since Dana is collapsing her colleague Matthew's "yup" with her husband's "yup," it is more critical than ever that she do some clearing to create emotional distance between she and her colleague Matthew so that she doesn't inadvertently bring her home life into the office situation. My suggestion is that Dana do some preparation by journaling, including making a list of all the ways in which her work situation with Matthew is different from her personal situation with her husband. Then I recommend she make a list of all the possible meanings Matthew's "yup" could have. (She would be wise to do the same for her husband's "yups" as a separate exercise.)

Next, Dana must rehearse how she is going to respond when she receives the next "yup" from Matthew. She may need to anchor to an object on her body to remember to remain neutral and take a deep breath before responding (see Chapter 4). In her rehearsal, she should follow these steps: First, connect with her anchor (an accessory or body part) as a reminder to choose a response rather than simply react. Second, take a deep breath or two. Third, recall as many of the things as she can from her list of what Matthew might mean. Fourth, ask him to share more specifically what he meant by "yup."

I also suggest that Dana wait to approach this situation *the next time it occurs* rather than initiating a discussion of a time it happened in the past. If Matthew is doing it inadvertently, he likely won't recognize the dynamic when she describes it to him and he might be defensive thinking she is analyzing the minutia of everything he says. Accordingly, Dana must wait for the next occurrence of "yup" or its equivalent to come from Matthew. When it does, from a place of neutrality and objectivity, Dana will go through her preparation sequence (anchor, breathe, remember) and then ask something along the lines of: "Say a little more about what you mean by that. There are several ways I could interpret it." If that isn't sufficient and she doesn't take her up on it, she might add "Like, maybe you already knew that and were annoyed with me for suggesting it, or maybe you didn't know it and were glad for the advice, or maybe something else entirely."

If Matthew simply agrees with her and is glad for the guidance, he may say so: "Yep, I got it. Thanks for the additional details." Or, he may give a more ambiguous answer, such as, "Yep, I got it. No big deal." Here's where Dana needs to determine whether there is sufficient trust and respect in the relationship to continue on this course and probe further. She might say, "Okay, I'm glad you've got it . . .and I'm trying to determine if you'd like me to continue to give you tips like that. If you don't, it's okay. It's just that your tone of voice suggests that I'm annoying you when I share those kind of tips." If there is sufficient trust and respect, Matthew will honestly tell her if he is annoyed or not.

If there is not sufficient trust and respect in the relationship or if Dana's remarks have triggered defensiveness, Matthew might come back with something like, "So what's your problem?" If that is the case, then it is likely Matthew's passive-aggressive behavior is indeed a front for the aggression that lies beneath it. He may be angry that he needs help, he might be threatened that a woman is helping him, or myriad other reasons. It is not Dana's place to figure out what is causing the aggression. She is best to take the situation to her manager and suggest that the dynamics between she and Matthew are not conducive to the mentoring relationship and that perhaps there is someone else on the team he could learn from.

CONCLUSION

This chapter addressed communication strategies employees and managers can use to discuss petty, yet disruptive, behaviors. Any of the situations in this chapter (or their cousins) taken individually as one-off behavior are quite mundane. It is tempting to ignore them and carry on. This approach often boomerangs, however. Sure, you may say that you're not going to let the mundane things get to you, because you "don't sweat the small stuff." However, if it is a recurring situation, you may go from thinking it's mundane to having it drive you insane in a flash. Better to address it as soon as you see a pattern and while it is still small than when it boomerangs back to you as a much larger issue.

In the next chapter, we turn to taking a head on approach to giving continuous feedback in informal settings and giving feedback in the more formal context of performance evaluations. But first, do the exercises below to lock in your understanding of the concepts in this chapter.

EXERCISES

#19: Communicating in Common Spaces

Look for a situation in a common space, either at work or at home. Find a relatively minor issue, but not one that has been bothering you for a long time. Maybe your child takes their socks off and leaves them in the family room. Or maybe a colleague nearby took a call on speakerphone in a public area today.

It's important to practice this skill on a relatively simple and straightforward situation rather than a complicated issue that's been bothering you for a long time. Think of it like riding a bike. If you're just learning to ride a bike for the first time, you do so on a relatively flat stretch of open space with smooth pavement, like an empty parking lot. You don't start on a busy street in rush hour. You will someday be able to ride there, but those are not the best circumstances under which to master the basics of riding. The same goes with learning to address the situations that can go from mundane to insane. And, as a bonus, if you approach them when they are mundane and resolve them, they will never become large enough to make you insane.

Approach that situation head on with the techniques you've learned in this chapter. Write down the techniques you will use to open the conversation and keep it on track.

#20: Eliminating Passive-Aggressive Behavior

Are you passive-aggressive? Use this checklist to find out. And, if you find that you are guilty of any of these passive-aggressive techniques, bring your awareness to them and eliminate them.

1. Saying yes when you mean no. Agreeing because you want to be a team player, when you in fact disagree, isn't noble. Stop it.

2. Overusing the word "Actually." When you use the word "actually," you are evading taking the issue head on. Consider this example: "This is actually a design the client might like." Translation: "I didn't think you were capable of producing a design they would like and I am pleasantly surprised."

3. Saying "I thought you understood . . ." As in "I thought you understood the deadlines were flexible" when you learn that your co-worker stayed up to the wee hours of the morning working to meet a fictional deadline. It's demeaning and disparaging. Instead, explain the deadlines matter-of-factly. And apologize.

4. Delivering a "softened message" with feigned surprise or confusion. The other person can see through it. This tactic is a roundabout way of being critical. If you disagree, share your disagreement straight up.

If you recognized yourself in any of these situations, you have some work to do. Remember, being straightforward with people builds trust and respect and strengthens relationships.

CHAPTER 11

Performance Evaluations and Continuous Feedback

Sophie was stunned. She'd just hung up the phone after her annual review with her manager, Rachel. Rachel, the new vice president of the division, was stationed at the headquarters of the manufacturing conglomerate and had been Sophie's manager for just three months. Sophie had been in her role as senior director of supply chain at one of the manufacturing plants for four years and was newly reporting to Rachel. Sophie had been very close with her previous manager, Carlos, but she had a good feeling about Rachel. She was excited to have a female manager and looked forward to being mentored by her in the future.

Performance evaluations with Carlos had always been *pro forma*. Not much meaningful information was exchanged. Sophie was an above average performer and managed supply chain extremely well. If there was something Carlos thought Sophie could improve upon, he came to her with it right away rather than saving it for her performance evaluation. As Sophie reflected on the conversation with Rachel, she realized she and Carlos had not had one of those constructive conversations in a long while.

Carlos had been working on a promotion for nearly a year and hadn't been as attentive to Sophie as he worked the corporate channels to secure a more senior level position.

The performance review with Rachel did *not* go as Sophie expected. In fact, it ended early at Sophie's request. Rachel began with a relatively incomplete picture of Sophie's project work from the past year, which immediately put Sophie on the defensive, trying to bring all of her accomplishments to the table without sounding desperate. Following that, Rachel discussed several opportunities for Sophie's professional growth, something Carlos had never done during the performance evaluation. Rachel was direct and professional, but between being in the formative stages of their relationship (they'd not yet met in person) and with receiving incomplete acknowledgement of her achievements and what felt like a laundry list of areas for improvement, Sophie was in full-on flight mode. Her defenses were up and she was simply unable to listen to Rachel and comprehend what she was saying.

"Rachel," Sophie interjected when there was a natural pause in the conversation, "could we stop for today and continue my review tomorrow or later this week?"

"Oh," Rachel responded, sounding surprised. "Is everything okay?"

"No," Sophie replied. "Everything's not okay. You've shared some feedback that I wasn't expecting, and I don't feel like you have a full picture of my accomplishments for the year. I'm feeling very defensive right now."

"Well, I'm just about to get to the good stuff now," Rachel responded.

"Frankly, I don't think I could even absorb the good stuff right now," Sophie replied. And that's how they'd left the discussion.

Sophie's mind spun as she grappled with the incomplete list of accomplishments, fair but unexpected criticism, and that she'd just prematurely ended the conversation. She wondered if she'd done the right thing.

This chapter discusses receiving and giving performance feedback both in the context of annual performance evaluations and in exchanges of critical and constructive continuous feedback outside of a formal process. Performance evaluation conversations are one of the most potentially high-impact conversations that can occur between employee and supervisor all year. Employees are provided with benchmark data about their performance and can make positive changes based on what they learn, especially if the feedback is delivered well. On the other hand, when feedback is not shared sensitively, it may result in hurt feelings, mistrust, gossip, lack of engagement, and turnover. Addressing opportunities for improvement is imperative; not doing so allows poor performance to continue and negatively affects organizational culture.

Ongoing feedback throughout the year is just as important, perhaps more so. But when supervisors and managers feel uncomfortable about delivering that feedback, they often avoid holding those conversations. This chapter provides tools and techniques for more easily initiating these exchanges. The techniques are equally useful whether you're providing downward, upward, lateral, or cross-functional feedback. Whether you supervise others or not, you need to be capable of both delivering and accepting constructive criticism. We all do. And we need to be good listeners. Listening is at the heart of giving and receiving feedback. This chapter examines the conditions that must be met in the brain and the conversation so that feedback can truly be heard.

We will examine performance evaluation feedback from both the perspective of the manager who is providing the feedback and the employee who is receiving the feedback. While presumably everyone is in the latter category (even CEOs receive feedback from their boards), and only some are in the former category, it is still helpful for those who are not supervisors, or not yet supervisors, to understand the process of *giving* feedback. When you have some appreciation for what is occurring on the other side of the desk, you may view the entire conversation differently.

RECEIVING PERFORMANCE FEEDBACK

As we have learned from previous chapters, when the sympathetic nervous system is not overly aroused, when fear is at bay and the creative and innovative juices are flowing (in other words, the prefrontal cortex is online), people are more able to connect with and listen to others in a meaningful way. That's exactly the state of mind you want to be in when you are having your performance evaluation conversation with your manager.

The context of an annual performance review is trigger enough for some employees to become defensive before they've even entered their manager's office for the review meeting. If that describes you, you must do some work before that meeting to get yourself into a more receptive state of mind. Review the concepts in Chapter 4 to create some emotional distance and get yourself in a state of mind where you can be receptive to new information and information that may differ with your perceptions of your performance. To the extent possible, avoid urgent, upsetting, or difficult situations just prior to your review so that you can arrive on time, in a calm state, and ready to discuss your successes and challenges. Coming to the conversation free and clear of distractions will help both you and your manager in holding this critical conversation and getting the most from it.

In addition to coming to the conversation in a calm and open state of mind, come prepared by having reviewed both your self-evaluation and your manager's evaluation of your performance. A word about each of these is in order. In most organizations, employees are asked to complete a self-evaluation of their work for the previous year, including accomplishments, setbacks, and opportunities for improvement. The more realistic and comprehensive you are as you complete this task, the easier the conversation will go. That realism includes not just acknowledging your setbacks and opportunities, which some people have a tendency to minimize.

It also includes clearly and specifically outlining your accomplishments. Some employees underplay their accomplishments, thinking that they don't want to be boastful or that their manager "just knows" about all their successes. Assume your manager does not know everything. Your manager is a busy person and he or she may have forgotten some of your smaller accomplishments (and sometimes your big ones too). Don't take it personally. Remember that they are human and that means they are prone to error just like everyone else. Your manager may have many direct reports to keep track of. So come prepared by having done a fair and accurate self-assessment. And if for some reason, your organization does not formally request that you do this as part of the evaluation process, do it yourself and share it with your manager.

Secondly, in most organizations, your manager will have prepared a written review of your performance for the year and shared it with you in advance of your performance evaluation meeting. Take the time to review that document in advance of the meeting. If there is feedback you weren't expecting, it will serve you well to have your initial reaction to that new information prior to the meeting with your manager. You might feel surprised, angry, frustrated, righteous, indignant, or have any number of other reactions to your manager's written comments. Having those reactions in front of your manager will not show you in your most professional light. Best to have that initial reaction away from your manager and as far before the meeting as possible.

The Meeting (Employee's Perspective)

How you carry yourself during the meeting can have an impact on how you are perceived as a professional. If you can calmly discuss areas for improvement without getting defensive or becoming overly emotional, your professionalism will be appreciated and noticed. Awareness of your default reactions to constructive and critical information can help you manage your emotions better during the meeting. For example, when constructive feedback is shared with you, do you typically get defensive? Angry? Indignant or righteous? Prone to tears? Or do you check out of the conversation, perhaps smiling on the outside while seething on the inside? The more awareness you have of your default reaction, the better you will be able to manage that reaction if it does occur.

Throughout the conversation, maintain a stance of objective inquiry (see Chapter 6). When you hear feedback that is unexpected, critical, constructive, or otherwise difficult for you to hear, make sure you know precisely what it means. Ask questions, ask for examples of your behavior, and ask what success looks like. Then, take note of any gaps. When you hear something you weren't expecting, take a curious stance rather than a defensive stance and ask for an example. You might say something like, "Hmm, I wasn't aware that I do that. Can you give me a specific example so I can think about it more carefully and pay attention to similar situations in the future?" Then, get ready to take notes. You might get defensive when you hear the example or the specifics of the feedback. Taking notes can help you put some emotional distance between the feedback and your response to it. It also gives you a reason to look down at your notebook and avoid making eye contact, which can help if you are struggling to remain composed.

Be prepared in the event you do get defensive in the meeting. It happens sometimes, despite the best attempts for it not to. Remember that it is okay to take a break during the meeting. It is perhaps a bit unconventional but perfectly acceptable for you to tell your manager that you've heard some surprises and that you are feeling defensive. Stating that you'd like to take a break and come back to the meeting in a less defensive state, as Sophie did at the beginning of this chapter, will demonstrate maturity and self-awareness on your part. On the other hand, if you continue with the meeting in a defensive state, your defensiveness might be mistaken for belligerence, arrogance, or any number of perceptions that will likely not reflect well on you.

Filter for Coaching

It's inevitable that you hear information about things you did wrong, or could do better. The person delivering the news could tear you down or build you up with constructive criticism. Even when you are aware of a shortcoming, it can be hard to hear it from another person. If you hadn't recognized an error or inadequacy, the information can trigger your defenses very quickly. When you receive negative feedback, pause before reacting. It is okay for there to be some silence in the meeting and for you to reflect on what is being shared.

When you hear information that feels critical or constructive, consider that it is being shared to coach you toward overall improved performance rather than being punitive in nature. I call this filtering for coaching. As your brain sorts through the new information, assume a bias toward thinking that this information is being given to you from a generous place that will help you be a better employee. In short, remind yourself that this information is meant to coach you toward being a stronger contributor in the organization. Another way to think about this is to assume positive intent. Your manager means well and is working to convey important information that will help advance your career.

When you are given feedback or suggestions that you don't agree with, which inevitably will happen, give your manager the benefit of the doubt and try them out. Consider that your manager sees your performance, your subject matter expertise, and your interactions with others from a different angle than you do. They may be shining a light on a blind spot for you. Try on their suggestions for doing things differently as if you were trying on a new pair of shoes. At first the shoes may feel stiff and uncomfortable, but after you walk in them a bit, you will be better able to determine whether they are a good fit for you. So too with constructive suggestions; they sometimes fit better than we expected them to.

As the meeting ends, recap any specific action items you've committed to doing or trying. They might come readily to mind or you may choose to request a follow up meeting for creating an action plan. In that case, you might say something like, "I'd like to meet again next week after I've had a chance to fully digest what we've talked about today. I want to put together an action plan to address the opportunities we discussed and I'd like to get your feedback on that. How about I put some time on your calendar for next week for us to have that conversation?"

Finally, thank your manager for their frank feedback and let them know that you've not only heard the feedback but that you've heard the spirit with which they shared it (provided you feel like they are coming from a place that has your best interests in mind). At the end of this chapter is a checklist to follow as you prepare for your review.

GIVING PERFORMANCE FEEDBACK

Much like the employee receiving the feedback, you as the manager will want to come to the performance evaluation conversation free and clear of any emotional distractions. Remember, those distractions may have nothing to do with the employee (i.e., family or personal situations, organizational politics, your own performance review) or they may have everything to do with the employee (how you think they are going to react, how they reacted last year, etc.). It can help if you develop a routine or ritual that puts you in a clear and positive state of mind before all of your performance evaluation meetings. Review some of the clearing techniques from Chapter 4 to help ensure that you bring your very best to the conversation, in service to the individual employee, the work team they are part of, and the organization.

Recall too, that some employees may be predisposed toward defensiveness and may arrive at the meeting tense and on edge. As the manager, it is your job to read the nonverbal and social cues that your employees project during the review meeting and account for them in the conversation. If an employee seems particularly nervous or upset before you've even begun, address that and try to make them feel at ease before continuing. It might sound something like this, "I know these conversations can be awkward sometimes. Nobody particularly likes to hear what they could be doing better. I feel the same way when I have my meeting like this with my boss.

My aim here is to have an open, honest conversation with you that has your best interests and the company's best interests in mind. How does that sound?" Of course, only say that you feel the same way in your performance evaluation if you actually do. If not, find another way to show vulnerability and make the employees feel at ease. By being vulnerable, you help to off-set the difference in power between the two of you and put the employee at ease. Whatever example you choose, make sure it is authentic.

Throughout the conversation, focus on reading the mind in the eyes of the employee. The more social sensitivity you have in the conversation, the easier it will be for the employee to hear what you have to say, especially the critical and constructive parts. If an employee seems to be getting defensive, it is perfectly okay to take a break in the conversation. Excuse yourself to go to the restroom or get a glass of water. There is no need to call attention to the employee's defensiveness unless they are having an extreme reaction (i.e., crying or shouting). In that case, it is perfectly okay to say, "Let's continue this conversation tomorrow. It's important that we have a frank discussion about this and that will be easier if we have a fresh start." Above all, avoid placing blame on the employee for having a reaction. Allow them to save face. Otherwise, they may have an even more intense reaction (i.e., become angrier or more defensive and even less receptive to your feedback).

There are two avoidable missteps managers often make when it comes to performance review conversations: being ambiguous and failing to provide enough information, particularly as it relates to critical and constructive feedback.

First, let's look at ambiguity. Let's suppose your employee's attire is not as professional as your organization requires, specifically when meeting with clients. Some managers will say something along the lines of, "It's important to look professional on days when our clients come to the office." This is ambiguous and unhelpful. Do not assume that an employee would connect that remark with their specific attire. After all, they think their clothing choices are perfectly appropriate for the office, otherwise they would be making other choices. If you are not specific with them that you are referring to their exact clothing choice, they will simply nod in agreement and not change their behavior at all. Instead, be specific, such as, "On days when we have clients visiting the office, it is important that you dress more professionally. Please consult the employee handbook after this meeting and review the dress code. Also, remember that all client meetings are scheduled in advance in the company calendar so you can look ahead to the next day to see if clients will be visiting and dress accordingly."

If you are doing a good job of using your social sensitivity skills, as I'm sure you are, you might notice a blank look from your employee or an air of confusion. Don't let that pass unnoticed. This is a perfect time to provide a specific example such as, "For example, last week we had a client in on Tuesday and you were wearing ripped jeans and a tee shirt." Of course, an attentive manager would have addressed the situation on Tuesday as it happened rather than saving it up for the performance evaluation. Inevitably though, you will have an employee whom you have given feedback to in the moment but the requested behavior change did not occur. In that case, you will find yourself discussing it again at the annual performance evaluation.

The second misstep managers often make is not providing enough information. In most cases, the subject you are about to broach is one you've given considerable thought to, sometimes obsessively so. The employee, on the other hand, has likely not thought much about this topic, if at all. Sometimes this consideration, thinking and strategizing in advance of the meeting, results in managers having synthesized the issue. Accordingly, they may include insufficient detail for the employee to fully grasp the gravity of the situation. One senior leader I worked with, who was by nature very concise and who thought long and hard before bringing issues up with employees, regularly did not provide enough detail when sharing constructive feedback with his direct reports. He overlooked their need for concrete examples of the areas in which they could improve.

Next, we turn to look at the ratio of positive to negative feedback needed for optimal behavior change. A good place to begin is by assessing the employee's level of expertise.

Novice or Expert?

Consider where your employees are on the learning curve in the area you're giving feedback. If they are novices, they will need a blend of positive feedback with critical feedback in order to stay motivated. They need to know specifically which areas of their job they have mastery over (or are reasonably good at) and which areas they should fine tune their approach or sharpen their skills. If they are new, whether to the organization, the role, or the specific area of feedback you are sharing, you will help to encourage and motivate them by sharing the positive feedback with the constructive feedback.

On the other hand, if they have amassed a certain amount of expertise, they will have less need for positive feedback. Constructive feedback will be sufficient to motivate them to improve their performance. Note that these are generalities and your individual employees may differ somewhat from the norm. Note also that there is not a single employee who does not need any positive feedback. We all like to hear that we are doing our jobs well, so don't skip the positive feedback entirely because you think the person doesn't need it. Note too, that this is different from praising someone for simply doing their job, like showing up on time. If there really is no good news and no demonstrated mastery of new skills during the past year, it is time for closer supervision and a corresponding improvement plan.

If you find yourself with direct reports who have reported to you for a long period of time, you may feel like there is not much left to say. Again, that falls under the category of "not enough information," one of the most frustrating things that employees encounter during the review process. In that case, take the time to think more critically about the employee's performance. This isn't to say that you should be overly critical about things that are insignificant. Rather, think longer term about the person's career track. Are there any skills they can begin to develop now to position them for the next step in their career?

I coached one senior executive on this who had had the same direct report for the past 15 years. The review was largely the same, year in and year out. There was no chance of his direct report moving up in the ranks because of her level of education and the size of the organization. During the performance evaluation, the senior leader addressed that directly and they talked about whether the direct report wanted to remain at that level for the rest of her career or if she would like the senior leader to coach her on getting the education and skills needed to move to a higher level, presuming she would find that next role elsewhere. Regardless of the specifics of the situation, if you've given the employee countless performance reviews over the years, find something new to say.

DEALING WITH DEFENSIVENESS

Sometimes, employees may get defensive during a performance review despite your best efforts. Here are a few techniques to use to recover the conversation and restore a sense of emotional safety for the employee.

Contrast

When an employee misinterprets feedback, use contrast to clarify. When using contrast, state what you think the employee heard, followed by what you wanted them to hear. It sounds something like this, "I don't want you to think that you aren't able to effectively work with clients. Certainly, you are. I do want you to understand that if you want to be promoted to the client advisor role, you will need to communicate more effectively with clients. That means . . ."

Another way to use contrast is to specifically state what you didn't mean and what you did mean. For example, "I didn't mean to imply that you aren't creative. What I meant was that you need stronger prose in the creative briefing documents for your creative ideas to come across well."

Here are a couple of templates for structuring contrast:

- "I *don't* want you to . . .. I *do* want you to . . .."
- "I *didn't mean* to imply that . . ..; *what I meant* was . . .."

What I See

Body language is often a better indicator of people's moods and attitudes than their words are. Human beings are much more likely to have their nonverbal communication give them away than their words. If the employee's words don't match their body language, including their expressions, posture, or tone, use this mirroring technique to share that inconsistency. To use the "What I See" technique, repeat what the person said (a summary or paraphrase is sufficient) and then describe the nonverbal behavior you are observing that carries a different meaning than what they've said. It might be something that you visually observe or it may be something you audibly pick up on. For example, "You say you are not upset and that you understand what I'd like you to do differently next time, but the tone of your voice sounds upset." Another common inconsistency is when an employee utters that something is "Fine" but by the tone of their voice, it is clearly anything but fine. This is another good time to use the "What I See" technique: "You say you are fine with the decision but your arms are crossed and your tone of voice suggests you are not in agreement."

Paraphrase

Rephrasing an employee's sentiment, sharing it back with them, and asking if you've correctly understood is an excellent way to show that you, in fact, do understand their position. It is also an effective technique in reducing defensiveness. The brain cannot easily hold agreement and defensiveness simultaneously. If you've paraphrased what the employee shared and then asked if you've gotten it correct, the employee will become less defensive because they are agreeing with you. It sounds like this, "Let me see if I understand. You're dissatisfied with the rating on written communication skills and you don't feel that the rating you received accurately reflects your performance this year. Is that right?" If you haven't understood them correctly, paraphrasing and double checking your comprehension is a great way to clear up any misunderstandings that you may have.

Priming

If you feel as if you are stuck or getting nowhere, try priming. Much like priming a pump, where you add water to get water, you put forward a hypothesis about what the employee might be thinking or what their reaction might be. It sounds like this, "Are you thinking that . . .[insert what you think they might be concerned about]?" or "Are you thinking that maybe I don't care about . . .?" Priming is designed to get the employee talking. If they are shut down and un-communicative, it is difficult if not impossible to develop shared meaning and understanding.

Taking a Break

If all else fails, and your efforts to bring the person back from their defensive state have not worked, take a break and resume the conversation at a later time. Be sure to do this in a manner in which you are not making the person even more defensive and that allows them to save face, as discussed earlier in this chapter.

Concluding the Review Meeting

As the performance evaluation conversation comes to an end, there are three things to be mindful of. First, make sure your employee has an action plan for addressing their opportunities for improvement. Without an action plan, the discussion has simply been an uncomfortable conversation that will not yield any behavior change. Second, create a timeline in which you would like to see progress. This is ideally driven by the employee so that the timeline and expected behavior changes are realistic for them. Finally, thank the employee for their professionalism, especially if you've shared feedback that was difficult for them to hear.

As you prepare for performance review evaluations and the difficult conversations that inevitably are part of the process, review the checklist for managers at the end of the chapter. It includes many good reminders for what to do before, during, and after the performance evaluation.

CONTINUOUS FEEDBACK

The annual performance review should be, as Sophie's review with her former manager Carlos was in earlier years, *pro forma*. If employees are receiving regular feedback, both positive and constructive, throughout the year, there should be no surprises at an end-of-year conversation. Even the challenging topics will not be as uncomfortable to discuss since they've been brought up before.

Once your organization has achieved a state of being open and receptive to continuous feedback, difficult conversations will not be so, well, difficult.

Creating a culture of continuous feedback is straightforward but it is not necessarily easy. It will take dedication and work. It is best accomplished not merely as top-down effort, but rather with support and involvement at all levels of the organization. There are five critical things that need to shift for an organization to create a culture of continuous improvement:

- Employees and leaders alike will need to become more responsive, willing to address issues immediately as they arise.

- They will need to be direct, which for many organizations means rooting out a culture of passive-aggressive behavior.

- Feedback must flow in all directions, not just downward.

- There must be a balance between positive and negative feedback within the organization; a culture of solely negative feedback is demoralizing.

- The organization must have a growth mindset that is oriented toward improvement and believes it is possible.

Let's take a look at each of these in greater detail.

Responsive

The days of saving feedback for the annual performance evaluation are long gone, especially if you want to have a culture that thrives on continuous improvement. Employees and supervisors alike need to be ready to give feedback—positive or negative—in the moment the behavior occurs, or as soon thereafter as is feasible. This is particularly effective when sharing constructive feedback. The details of the event or behavior you are giving feedback on are far crisper, both for you and for the employee receiving the feedback.

When you are able to pull someone aside and have a private conversation with them immediately, it also impresses upon them the importance of the feedback. The more time that passes before the issue is addressed, the less perceived importance the issue has and accordingly, the less impact your feedback will have. If changing behavior is your goal, place the feedback as close in time to the event as possible. This is not limited to constructive feedback. If you want to reinforce positive behavior, sharing it as quickly as possible will also ensure it has the most benefit.

Giving feedback in the moment also builds trust. It demonstrates that you have the person's professional development in mind and that you want to see them working toward fulfilling on the organization's mission to the best of their ability. It also shows your respect for the person. Not only are you *not* saving it up for their performance review, you hold them in high enough esteem to know they can handle the feedback and that they will use it wisely. Again, this goes for both positive and constructive feedback.

Direct

To provide effective feedback efficiently and effectively in the moment, you will need to be direct. Using ambiguous language or passive-aggressive communication will not yield the results you want. Use the techniques outlined in Chapter 10 to eradicate your own passive-aggressive tendencies if you have them and to address passive-aggressive behavior when your colleagues are using it.

Being direct also means being specific. As we've discussed above, ambiguous or unclear feedback is ineffective at changing behavior. In fact, it can do more harm than good. When you dance around or hint at feedback, especially constructive feedback, but do not share it openly, your employee or colleague will sense to some degree that there is an issue that you'd like to address. If you are not direct about it, there will be an intimation of distrust at some level, even a minor level. They will know you have something to say but will not be sure of your motives for not saying it, thus inviting suspicion and distrust.

If you aren't getting feedback, don't wait. Instead, request it and direct it. Make specific requests from those you wish to receive feedback from. Direct them toward the particular area you are hoping to improve upon. Instead of asking, "Do you have any feedback for me?" ask, "What's one thing you see where I could be more efficient when conducting an audit?" Be ready to direct the conversation further, especially if you aren't getting feedback in the area you requested. You might say, "I appreciate your comments on my internal communication, however, I'm more interested in how I can be more efficient when performing an audit with a client, especially during our peak season."

Multidirectional

In order to become an organization that supports continuous improvement through feedback, the feedback must flow in all directions, not just top down. It must be the norm for colleagues to share feedback with one another laterally. Likewise, managers and supervisors must be open and receptive when receiving feedback from those who report to them. This needs to be the case from the to the top of the organization to the most junior level supervisors.

Often it is the most junior level supervisors who have the most difficult time receiving feedback from those who report to them, especially when it is constructive. More senior managers and executives on the other hand, have had an entire career's worth of experience handling feedback and are more accustomed to it. Further, the closer to the top of the organization one gets, the more one is vested in how the organization as a whole is doing, since that is considered a direct reflection of a senior leader's performance (not to mention their compensation package is typically tied to the company's performance). More junior level managers and supervisors, on the other hand, typically have their own interests in mind and want to know they are doing well as a supervisor, especially if they are new to the job. They haven't had as much experience receiving feedback in their role and may be predisposed to getting defensive as a result.

The best way to encourage feedback in all directions—down, up and lateral—is for senior leaders to demonstrate their receptivity to feedback and their willingness to act on it. As senior leaders show that they can receive feedback graciously, their example can cascade down the leadership chain as their direct reports demonstrate openness to their own staff, and so on. The most coaching will be needed by those who are newest to managing the work of others and to those who are giving and receiving feedback from their peers.

Balanced

When critical feedback is given without positive feedback, especially when it is potentially coming from any and all directions, it is not likely to motivate employees effectively. Positive feedback needs to remain part of the mix and be shared regularly. Providing positive feedback will go a long way toward making constructive feedback more palatable, especially when sharing feedback laterally. Providing balance is qualitatively different from the sandwich method described in Chapter 5. Rather than slipping the critical feedback in between two positive comments, balance is achieved when positive and constructive feedback are both shared periodically, but not necessarily in the same setting. If a colleague only shares when there is something critical to say, it will be frustrating and demoralizing to hear their feedback. Like a high-performing sports team, there must be regular "atta-boy" and "atta-girl" exchanges to reinforce good work across the organization and the sense of appreciation that is carried in those positive sentiments.

Growth Oriented

Without a philosophy that supports growth and development, it will be difficult for your organization to maintain a culture of continuous improvement. Researcher Carol Dweck distinguishes between a growth mindset and a fixed mindset and has spent her career understanding the difference between the two.[28] When people believe their basic qualities and abilities can be developed or improved through effort and dedication they have what Dweck refers to as a growth mindset. On the other hand, if they believe their basic qualities and abilities like their intelligence or talent are fixed traits (i.e., difficult or impossible to change), they have a fixed mindset. People with a fixed mindset often believe that talent alone creates success (without effort). They spend their time proving their skills and intelligence instead of developing them.

In order to develop a growth mindset in your organization, you will need a balance of constructive feedback and positive feedback as described above. But not just any praise will do in developing a growth mindset. In one of their studies, Dweck and her colleagues investigated the impact that praise had on children's development. Four hundred fifth grade students from across the United States were given an assessment to measure their general intelligence, or IQ. At the end of the test, all the children were given praise, but they were praised in two different ways. The first group was praised for their intelligence and those students were specifically told they were smart. Students in the second group were praised for their effort and for how hard they worked on the test. This may seem like a subtle difference but the impact it had was anything but subtle.

Next, the children were given options with regard to the test they would like to take next. The first option was described as a little harder and an opportunity to learn and grow. The second option was described as a fairly easy test that they would very likely do well on. Here's where the research gets interesting. Of the group that was praised for their intelligence, two thirds chose the easy test as their next test. Meanwhile, 92 percent of the children who were praised for their effort chose the *more difficult* test. The subtle difference in how they were praised made all the difference in the degree of challenge they were willing to take on next.

As Dweck explains, the person who is praised for their intelligence assumes that they are valued for their intelligence and that they had better not perform in a way that will negate that evaluation. As a result, they play it safe, wanting to live up the expectations others have of them and they enter a fixed mindset. In so doing, they limit their personal and professional growth. Alternatively, by focusing on how much effort a person puts forth, commenting on the strategies the person used, and the way they are rising to the challenge of more complex tasks, the emphasis is on the process of growth. As a result, people are more willing to take risks and work hard because they are oriented toward growth and want to continue to grow.

Next the kids were given another test, an extremely difficult test. The researchers wanted to see if and how the kids who were praised for their effort would respond differently from those who were praised for their intelligence. Those who were praised for their effort worked longer, demonstrated more effort and reported enjoying the activity more than those who were praised for their intelligence. In fact, the group who was praised for their intelligence became frustrated easily and had a tendency to give up. In the final round of testing in the experiment, the children were given a test that was the same level of difficulty as the first test. Those who were initially praised for their intelligence did worse on this test. Their average score dropped by an astounding 20%. Meanwhile, the group who was praised for their effort initially, did better. A lot better. Their scores rose by nearly 30%. This is a 50% difference in average score resulting from how they were praised.

This study shows that not all praise is created equal. If you want to develop an organization that is oriented toward continuous feedback that makes a difference, not only do you need to include positive feedback, you need to be acutely aware of how that feedback is delivered so that it cultivates a growth mindset.

CONCLUSION

The secret to becoming an organization that embraces continuous feedback is for every member of the organization to adopt an attitude of responsiveness, directness, openness to feedback from multiple directions, a willingness to provide both positive and negative feedback, and a growth mindset. And finally, when feedback comes your way, filter for coaching. Think of the feedback as having your best interests and the best interests of the organization in mind. If everyone in the organization can do that, at least most of the time, your organization will thrive.

EXERCISES

#21: Review Preparation Checklist, Employees

Use this checklist to prepare for your performance review meeting with your manager.

- ❑ The day before your evaluation, review your Self Evaluation, your last review, and any other relevant documentation that may be referenced during the performance evaluation meeting.
- ❑ Consider areas of your performance in which your manager may have constructive feedback. Be ready to discuss them in a non-defensive manner.
- ❑ Get a good night's sleep.
- ❑ Take a brisk walk or participate in another form of exercise if you regularly do so.
- ❑ Keep your schedule relatively light in the one or two hours immediately prior to your review.
- ❑ Visualize the conversation being a productive, constructive session that leaves you challenged and invigorated.
- ❑ Arrive on time.
- ❑ Immediately before your review, take a few deep breaths.
- ❑ Manage defensiveness as it comes up during the review through breathing and anchoring.
- ❑ Take a break if you find yourself overly defensive.
- ❑ Take notes throughout the review, especially on areas where constructive feedback is shared.
- ❑ Ask for specific examples for anything you don't understand or aren't sure of (remember to ask from an objective, curious stance rather than a defensive one).
- ❑ Make a follow up plan for addressing shortcomings and opportunities or put a meeting on the calendar to discuss them in the short term.
- ❑ Thank your manager for their candor and the spirit in which they shared the feedback.

#22: Review Preparation Checklist, Managers

Use this checklist to prepare for your performance review meeting with each employee.

- ❏ Do **not** use the "sandwich" method (see Chapter 5 for details).
- ❏ Be direct.
- ❏ Balance authenticity with diplomacy.
- ❏ Be specific.
- ❏ Be transparent.
- ❏ Make it collaborative; a conversation.
- ❏ Check in frequently to gauge how the feedback is landing.
- ❏ Make a practice of reading the body language of your employee and adjust or ask questions accordingly.
- ❏ Balance feedback between evaluative feedback (i.e., "Your score is 'Meets Expectations.'" or "Your score is a 4.") and coaching feedback ("Here are some techniques you might try as you work toward managing your time better when wrapping up projects.")
- ❏ Get feedback on your feedback.
- ❏ Thank your employee for their receptiveness to your feedback.

Use this space to jot down specific strengths or weaknesses you plan to discuss.

CHAPTER 12

Communicating Effectively with Senior Leaders

Yolanda, a part-time accountant wasn't long in her new job with a non-profit when something didn't add up. Literally. She couldn't reconcile the payroll account. A natural problem solver, Yolanda investigated. She looked at her predecessor's records and they didn't add up either. Money was missing each month. It wasn't a lot, but it was money. Yolanda's job was to account for the money. She continued her search, looking in other accounts and finding more and more situations that simply didn't add up.

Until they did.

Yolanda discovered, through her detailed research, that Alex, the payroll clerk, was skimming money from the accounts. Alex seemed very close with Ian, Yolanda's manager. Yolanda knew she needed to tell someone, and quickly. Given the close relationship between Ian and Alex, Yolanda decided to involve Ian's manager, the Controller, as well. She scheduled a meeting with the two of them.

When you need to have a difficult conversation with your boss or a senior leader in your organization, the stakes are high and in most cases, there is a real cost to a failure to connect, be that a cost in your perceived value to the organization, your reputation, or in some cases, your advancement opportunities and your career itself. Whether your manager is making a bad decision, you messed up (badly!) or something personal like a major health or relationship issue is standing between you and your best work performance, you will need to have a conversation about a difficult topic with your manager or a senior leader in your organization at some point.

One of the most important career skills you can develop is knowing how to effectively bring a problem to the attention of your manager. Frequently, people handle such situations poorly and end up looking inept, insecure, or hostile. In this chapter, we aim to rectify that. The first half of the chapter looks at particularly high stakes situations in which someone has messed up, or is about to, including a leader. In the second half of the chapter, we look at how to communicate effectively with senior leaders in less stressful but still important situations.

The overarching message of the chapter is to get into action. It is easy to sit back on one's laurels, waiting for the perfect timing or for the situation to resolve itself, neither of which are likely to occur. Any of us has at one time hesitated to bring a difficult topic to light with a manager, especially if it involves contradicting a superior. But in fields where lives may literally be at stake—like medicine, aviation, and energy to name a few—clear and effective communication is imperative, especially when something goes wrong or a decision is questionable. Interestingly, these also seem to be the professions with the most rigid hierarchies, and those in which doubting superiors (whether in rank or direct reporting structure) is taboo. Regardless of your industry, this chapter will equip you with tools for communicating bad or difficult news upward and provide specific conversational tactics that create a safer environment for addressing such situations head on.

WHEN THE STAKES ARE HIGH

When the stakes are high and you need to initiate a difficult conversation, there's a good chance someone's made a big mistake or is about to. Let's make sure it's not you making the mistake during the conversation! Regardless of whose misstep it is, it's important to keep your focus on the solutions rather than the problems. We will look at how to handle a difficult situation with your manager when you're the cause of the problem, when a colleague is at fault, and when the manager is responsible for the mishap.

You've Messed Up

If you've made a blunder at work, especially one that costs the company customers, money, production time, or anything else that can be directly traced to the bottom line, you'll need to speak up quickly, take responsibility, and focus on how you will remedy the situation. Taking the issue head-on is imperative.

First, schedule a time to meet with your manager as soon as possible. If your manager is not in the office, plan to meet by phone or videoconference. Do not wait until he or she is back in the office. Time is of the essence and it will help that you didn't delay in sharing the news with them. They should be the first to know; pay them that respect and they will be likely to respect you as well. In the request to meet, share that the situation has urgency. A meeting subject line might be "Important update on the garden gnome project" and you might include an acknowledgement of their busy schedule or other competing priorities so that they know you view this discussion as urgent, given their current context.

When you meet, begin the conversation by immediately stating exactly what is wrong. Deliver the bottom line first. Managers and leaders have limited time and attention. They want you to get right to the point. When you are communicating with your manager and the senior leaders in your organization, you are not sharing a mystery story in which it all makes sense in the end. Don't make them guess and don't make them follow a plot with many twists and turns. They don't have the patience for it. Rather, begin with your conclusions and then use the rest of your time to support those conclusions with data, your rationale, and other evidence you need to share for them to understand the situation.

Additionally, make sure you are taking responsibility for what has occurred if you were at fault in the matter. This is not the time to pass the buck on a colleague or be vague or ambiguous. Demonstrating ownership of the problem will increase the respect that your manager has for you. Shirking that responsibility will do the opposite. In a difficult situation, especially one that you have caused or contributed to, dodging responsibility will damage the relationship and will not reflect well on you. Taking responsibility quickly and owning the unfavorable situation will lessen the damage to your professional reputation.

Let's suppose that an important deadline was missed because of your mishandling of a client account. The client will not get their shipment in time to meet their own production deadlines and now they have threatened to end their relationship with your company and become a customer of your top competitor. Start your conversation with your boss by saying something like, "The Rainbow Unicorn account is in jeopardy and they are threatening to take their business to the competition. I mishandled their latest order and they are upset."

You may choose to add a few more details, but only as many as your boss needs in order to quickly comprehend the situation. Being concise is important precisely because you want to spend more time discussing the solution than the problem. There may be a time to rehash what went wrong in greater detail later as part of a discussion about preventing recurrence of the problem, but for the initial conversation, the focus should be on quickly laying out the problem and then moving on to solutions.

It is important to present a solution paired with the problem. That demonstrates leadership, accountability, and responsibility for fixing the mess you've created. Sometimes the solution to the problem will be straightforward and you will know exactly what to propose. In other cases, you may feel as if you don't have a viable solution or don't know where to begin. Do not go to the meeting empty handed. Rather, come up with several potential solutions. After you've succinctly shared the problem, you'll say something along the lines of, "Given the situation, we could do A, B, C, or something that we devise together." In adding the last possibility, "something we devise together," you are positioning yourself as a problem-solver, even if you don't have a good solution to the problem in the present moment. It also positions you and your boss as a team in fixing what went wrong, especially in a case where you don't know the best solution.

Be prepared to listen closely and manage your defensiveness. Your boss may be wildly upset or incredibly understanding or anywhere in between. Managing your defensiveness and staying present will enable you to get the most out of the conversation, both in terms of comprehension and relationship development. As for comprehension, if you can remain present, listen, and ask good questions, you are more likely to reach an outcome that suits your boss than if you weren't fully engaged. Secondly, staying grounded and present in the discussion will demonstrate your professional maturity and will enable your manager to think of you more as a professional colleague rather than a screw up.

Create a plan of action once you have agreed up on the best solution. Summarize that plan of action before closing the conversation. Then, take action immediately. Your ability to respond quickly
and accurately in the face of a crisis, especially one that you caused,
is critical in building or rebuilding trust after a mishap.

A Colleague Messed Up

When a colleague makes a mistake, you'd like them to take personal
responsibility and share their errors and proposed solution with
their manager, but that doesn't always happen. Avoiding responsibility is not uncommon and if it happens, you might easily see the
risk of your colleague's inaction and want to take action yourself.
How can you diplomatically step up if your colleague shirks from
taking action?

If your colleague knows that you are aware of the situation, encourage them to bring the issue forward with leadership on their
own. Take a moment to connect with your colleague and encourage
them to take ownership. You might share how you've had similar
conversations with leaders in the past and that it has worked out
well, or encourage them that it is in the best interest of their career
to take responsibility for the situation. Do your best to be persuasive and have your colleague go forward with the issue before
meeting with a manager or senior leader yourself. The exception
would be a case where laws have been broken or there has been
intentional malfeasance, like the situation that Yolanda found herself in at the beginning of the chapter. Then it does make sense to
go straight to a manager or senior leader and bypass your colleague. These are rather rare circumstances.

If you do need to meet with your manager or senior leader to
bring the issue to their awareness, either because your colleague

has declined your invitation to take the issue forward themselves or because you believe there has been malicious intent or foul play, be succinct and direct as you would if it were your own mistake. There is no need to belabor the point. In addition, refrain from using blaming language as you recount the facts of the situation. The more clearly you can focus on the facts, the more highly you will likely be regarded by your manager for bringing the issue to their attention. When you keep shared goals and the best interests of organization clearly in focus rather than indicting your colleague, you will be more likely to be perceived as part of the solution rather than someone who ratted out their colleague.

During these conversations, refrain from using absolute language when referring to your colleague, such as "She *always* makes mistakes like these" or "He *never* takes responsibility for his actions." Using absolute language tends to lock you into a position where your natural tendency will be to fall into an "us against them" mentality. You may be prompted to defend your position, which makes you, well, defensive. Additionally, in locking into a position, you will set yourself up for a potential conflict that may transcend the current business problem and begin to feel personal. Absolute language tends to focus on the individual rather than the work or the business problems. With the Fact AND model and other strategies we've discussed, we are taking care to keep the focus on the issue at hand rather than the person. Keeping absolutes out of the conversation will help you remain professional.

As with situations where you caused the problem, when your colleague is at fault, focusing on and being part of the solution will fare better for you than dwelling on the problem. Keep the solution or potential solutions in the forefront as you discuss the situation with your manager and any other parties. In many cases, your colleague will eventually be brought into the discussion. You will help keep your colleague's defenses lower if you can keep the focus of the conversation on the solution. Again, there may be time later for a deeper dive into how the situation originated, but for now, keep the focus on the solution and the future.

As solutions are identified and implemented, you might then bring a more systemic approach to the issue by looking to see if there is a set of contributing variables that enabled the situation to unfold as it did. Yolanda, from the beginning of the chapter, could propose a series of checks and balances be put in place so that the payroll clerk, regardless of whether it was Alex or someone else, would not be able to skim a few cents from the accounts.

Your Leader Messed Up

Managers and leaders are human. From micromanaging to being unable to make a decision to moving forward with an ill-informed strategy, they show their humanity. When you are approaching your manager in a situation where they are at fault, it is important to keep that humanity in mind and to assume positive intent. Managers do not wake up and think to themselves, "How can I go into the office and impede the progress of my best employees today?" They just don't. Remembering that they most likely had a positive intent when they did what they did (or didn't do) will help you approach them tactfully and with humility.

To hold the discussion, set up the meeting as you would to discuss any other issue. When the meeting begins, use the Fact AND model, starting by stating shared goals and the good work of your team or division. Then, respectfully and graciously share the problem and how it is affecting you (i.e., your performance, your ability to be on board and in agreement, the direction of the team). If you felt your manager was micromanaging you, for example, you might start with something like this: "Talia, thanks for making time to meet with me today. You know how important the current market research project is, both to the success of the new product and to me professionally. I'd like to reduce the number of check-in meetings you and I have in order to give me more time to work on the substance of the project. I know it is important for you to be informed on a high-profile project like this. Could we talk about a balance that will meet your needs and be a bit easier on my schedule?"

Note that the word "micromanaging" was not used in the opening of this conversation. As you will recall from Chapter 5 when we discussed how to open a conversation without making the other person defensive, we emphasized that the specific words you select make a significant difference in how the other person reacts to what you say and whether or not they get defensive. By naming the specific behavior that the manager is doing (requiring frequent check-ins), we keep the focus on the behavior we wish to see changed. No one likes to be thought of as a micromanager, and so keeping that pejorative term out of the conversation serves both the conversation and the relationship.

Furthermore, whether it is a case of too many check-ins (micromanaging) or some other behavior that you raise with your manager, you may be shedding light on one of your manager's blind spots. Blind spots are areas or characteristics that are known to others but not known to ourselves. Because it is a blind spot or an area previously unnoticed or unrecognized, it will likely come as a surprise to your manager to learn this new information. It may also be the case that this new information is inconsistent with your manager's existing self-concept. This alone can prompt defensiveness, regardless of how well you opened the conversation.

The next part of the conversation is to remain open to what your manager's response might be. You'll need to keep your defensiveness in check during this portion of the conversation. Stay curious, listen closely to what your manager says in response, and ask follow-up questions. Your goal is mutual understanding and that will only come about through an active exchange of give and take, speaking and listening.

As the conversation comes to a close, work toward an agreement that includes a concrete plan for what will change. Are there periodic updates you can give your manager so that she doesn't need to meet with you as frequently? Are there other ways for your boss to get what he needs so that he doesn't need to interrupt you so often? As you sort these out, agree on which ones will serve the needs of both parties and articulate who will do what when.

When you get back to your office, send a brief email thanking your boss for their time and outlining the steps you both agreed to. This will make your agreement more tangible and your boss will have a chance to reflect and respond if there is anything that he or she disagrees with or thinks is different from what you discussed.

It is sensitive to bring up what are essentially your boss's shortcomings, especially if your organization does not have a culture that supports immediate and continuous feedback. In addition to structuring your conversation as we've outlined here, I suggest that you practice several times with a trusted friend or colleague before holding the conversation with your manager. Your practice partner can alert you to any words or turns of phrase that might make your boss defensive and the additional practice will help you feel more confident as you hold the conversation.

Not all situations will fall into the high-stakes category. Some conversations with your manager or senior leader may not be based on mistakes or missteps, but they may be awkward or difficult to discuss nonetheless. We cover those conversations next.

WHEN THE STAKES ARE MODERATE

Perhaps there has been no misstep or no mistake made, but you need to discuss an uncomfortable topic with your manager. The nature of the topic makes it a difficult one to bring up and you'd perhaps rather avoid the issue than address it. However, you know that if not addressed now, there is the potential for it to become a much larger issue over time. Or perhaps it is something that needs to be addressed immediately, like a resignation conversation, and there is no easy way to say what needs to be said.

Your Personal Life

Sometimes things happen in your personal life that may have a dramatic impact on your work performance, or the potential to do so. In most cases, you would do well to inform your manager of what is going on, even if it is a difficult subject to broach. Examples include having a significant medical problem that needs attention, a relationship dilemma with your significant other, caring for an aging parent or a sick child, or a disrupted living situation, perhaps moving or remodeling your home. In any of these situations, your ability to bring your best effort to your work every day is at risk. And, if you happen to experience more than one of these at a time (why do massively disruptive phenomena in one's personal life seem to happen all at once?), your ability to play full out at work will most certainly be compromised.

Although you may be inclined to want to keep your personal life private and not share it with others at work, least of all your manager, in situations like these it is imperative to share at least a few facts with your boss. Much as you might like to, you can't exactly check your emotions and your reactions to your personal life at the door when you step into the office. However, you can connect with your boss on the issue in a way that does not sound like you are complaining, asking for special favors, or asking your boss to solve your personal problems. And you can do so without sharing intimate details of your personal life.

Take into account whether your manager is more relationship or task focused. If she doesn't swing by to ask how you're doing on a regular basis or make small talk, there is a good chance she is more task focused. On the other hand, if she does stop by regularly to inquire about your family, what you did over the weekend, or chat about the weather or your favorite team's score in last night's game, she is probably more relationship focused. If you're not used to sharing personal information with your manager because one or both of you is more task focused, the conversation will most certainly feel awkward. You'll want to put special emphasis on the effect the situation may have on your work. On the other hand, if one or both of you is more relationship focused, the conversation might feel a bit more natural and you may be more comfortable disclosing additional information.

Let's say that your teenager has recently been diagnosed with an eating disorder and you need to take him for out-patient appointments with a nutritionist, a counselor, and a nurse practitioner on a weekly basis during business hours. If you are not comfortable sharing either the details or the diagnosis, you might say something like this to your manager, "Hey Adam, thanks for making time to talk with me on short notice. I wanted to let you know that my son has just received a medical diagnosis that requires me to take him to weekly doctor appointments during business hours for the next couple of months. I wanted to give you a head's up before you saw my "Out of Office" notifications come through. It looks to be something that will take a few months to get fully resolved. I don't expect it to impact my work performance, except for using some of my vacation time."

Or, let's suppose you have a relationship issue with your spouse or significant other. It isn't something that you anticipate will result in much time away from the office, but you know your level of concentration isn't what it normally is. You might share something like this with your manager: "Hey Adam, thanks for carving out a few minutes for us to talk. I've got a situation that I wanted to share with you on a high level. You know discretion is very important to me and I'd like you to keep this confidential. There's a little drama in my family life right now. I'd rather not share the details, but I wanted you to know that I'm doing my best to remain focused and engaged at work in the midst of it. I wanted to be proactive and let you know in case I seem a little distant or distracted from time to time. If it gets to a point where I need to take some personal time off to handle it, I certainly will do so."

Whether there is a medical issue, a relationship issue, or a logistics issue with you or with someone close to you that may impact your work, you're going to be better off if you address the issue proactively with your manager rather than reactively after it has negatively impacted your work. Even those who hold the strictest of boundaries between their personal and professional lives will find this to be the case.

It has two primary and positive benefits. First, your manager will be much more understanding if the situation outside of work does impact your work performance. Chances are, he or she has been in a similar situation at one point in their career and can empathize. It also makes it easier for them to bring your work performance up with you if it does suffer. Second, it puts you in control of the impression you are making on others. You choose the words and how much detail to share, and they see you as someone who is proactive and a hard worker, despite hurdles outside of work. You are proactively managing your career and your reputation.

Problems with a Coworker

You're not likely to get along swimmingly with all of your team-mates all of the time. Occasionally you are going to clash over something and once in a while, you might even feel out and out disdain for a coworker. You are the best judge as to whether it is something you can simply ignore and get over or whether it needs to be addressed. If it does need to be addressed, I can't stress enough how important it is to talk directly to your coworker, following the steps outlined in Section Two of this book. In most cases, it will strengthen the relationship between you and your coworker and you will feel confident in your ability to manage conflict successfully and reach agreement.

Occasionally however, the conflict between you and your coworker will eclipse your ability to successfully navigate the situation and you will need to get your boss involved. When you do so, be sure you've carefully thought through whether it is worth making this your boss's problem. That is essentially what you are doing if you choose to go to him or her with the issue. If you do take the issue up the chain of command to your manager, be sure to come with a solution in mind.

Let's say you're regularly assigned to work with Jess on projects. You are the person who is supposed to be the primary liaison with the client but Jess routinely goes directly to the client, cutting you out of the loop. On several occasions, this has left you feeling flustered when you've spoken with the client and found out that Jess had already filled them in on project details that you were calling to share. You've addressed it several times directly with Jess and you weren't able to reach a lasting agreement. When you go to your boss, say something along the lines of, "Jess and I are having a hard time coordinating communication with our clients. We've talked about it directly and the solutions we've come up with aren't working. I'd like to get your feedback and coaching first, and if that doesn't work, I'd like to be assigned to different projects from the ones Jess is working on."

While it might not be feasible for your boss to move you off the projects with your over-reaching colleague, it does bring the situation to light in a respectful manner which demonstrates that you've tried to address the issue yourself and you're coming with a solution to a problem, rather than just the problem itself. It also opens the discussion without condemnation or blaming of your colleague. Your boss may want to hear more about the situation and provide some coaching, so be ready to share specific examples while remaining fact-based, professional, and respectful.

Understand, too, that situations like these typically do not have easy answers. You may be bringing up an issue that is entirely outside of your boss's awareness, or it might be an issue that others have come to him with in the past. While there may not be a quick fix, allowing your boss in on the situation, does however, give him an opportunity to be on the lookout for the offending behavior so he or she can address it with your coworker directly, give you coaching on how to handle it differently, or implement the solution you suggested.

You're Leaving

Telling your boss you're moving on is typically a breeze if you loathe either your job or your boss or both. But when you've come to know, like, and respect your manager, giving notice can be excruciating. You may feel that your chances of remaining profession-al colleagues in your field will be dashed or that she will take it per-sonally. If you are moving on to something bigger and better, it's probably more likely that she is going to find the news bittersweet: sad to see you go, while also being thrilled to see your professional career growth. Regardless of her reaction, it's important to share the news in a way that does not damage the relationship.

Find a time to deliver the news as soon as possible. Be sure to tell your boss you are leaving before you share the news with your co-workers or anyone else in your organization. News of this nature travels fast and you will be hard pressed to be the first to share it with your manager if you've already told others in the organization. Plan for a brief face to face meeting if possible. If either you or your manager are traveling or if you don't work in the same physical lo-cation, then a phone call or videoconference will suffice.

Do not, I repeat, do not send the news by email or text message. It may be awkward and uncomfortable to look your manager in the eye and tell her you are leaving, especially if she has poured energy, resources, and care into your professional development. On the other hand, if you haven't enjoyed your role or reporting to your manager, you may have a fair amount of disdain for her. That doesn't change the fact that it is unprofessional to text or email your resignation. Take the high road one last time and tell her in person that you are moving on.

Find a time when your manager's stress levels tend to be low. Coming in a bit earlier than usual and catching her at the front end of the day often works well. Be gracious and professional, and add a personal touch if it feels right. If you've enjoyed working for your manager and feel heartsick about telling her you are moving on, the conversation might start something like this: "Eva, thanks for find-ing a few minutes for me to stop by this morning. You've been a mentor to me over these past five years at Rainbow Sunshine Corp., and I never imagined the day would come when I'd be moving on. Yesterday I accepted the position of Head of the Project Management Office at the Intergalactic Zoo. Your coaching and development helped me land this role and I'm so grateful. I want to work closely with you and the others in our group over these next couple of weeks to make sure that this transition is as smooth as possible."

On the other hand, if you've not enjoyed working for your manager or the organization, do not sugar coat it. Still meet in person, be respectful and be professional. It might sound something like this: "Eva, thanks for finding a few minutes for us to meet this morning. I wanted to stop by personally and tell you this news. Yesterday I accepted the position of Head of the Project Management Office at the Intergalactic Zoo. I'm very excited about this new role, although I'll certainly miss [insert something you like about your current organization]. I want to work closely with you and the others in our group over these next few weeks to make sure that my transition is as smooth as possible for you and the rest of the team."

Another variation on the "I'm leaving" conversation might be that you're not leaving permanently but you do want to take some extra time away from the office for a "side hustle" you've got going. People take on side jobs for all sorts of reasons, some of them financial but oftentimes because the work is personally rewarding or uses a different skill set than does your day job. The time may come when you need to invest more time into that side hustle than usual and you won't want it to compromise your full-time gig. This could range from taking an extended period of time away from the office, to adjusting your work hours, or some other request.

Regardless of what the request is, share the facts, remain professional and be clear about what you are asking for. It might sound something like this: "Eva, thanks for taking a few minutes to meet with me this morning. As you know, I've long held a passion for cattle and I've been spending some of my time on nights and weekends grooming cattle for competitive showings. Bessie, one of the Red Angus that I groom, will be competing in the International Red Angus Show which is basically Westminster for cows. I've been asked to groom Bessie at the show and I plan to use my paid time off and take two weeks to attend the show later this fall. I'll work closely with the team to make sure nothing is missed while I am out."

CONCLUSION

Regardless of whether it is an uncomfortable topic or a high stakes situation, remember to keep your focus on the work and the organization. It is not personal, not for you nor for your manager. Odds are, your manager has had employees with circumstances that are equally if not more uncomfortable in the past. And, odds are that she has been in a similar dilemma at some point in her own career. Follow the method you've learned in this book for holding difficult conversations and the specific tips offered in this chapter and you will be on your way to delivering the news with grace and aplomb.

EXERCISES

#23: Owning Up

Think of a time when you had a high stakes situation that you need-ed to discuss with your manager where you were at fault. If you are lucky enough to have never had one, use your imagination or bor-row a situation that happened to a friend or colleague.

Using the techniques from this chapter, script how you would begin the dialogue. Be sure to demonstrate responsibility and ac-countability as well as pairing the problem with a solution.

#24: Personal Issues

Identify a time when your personal life was so demanding that it threatened the quality of your work at that point in your career. What exactly was happening and how was it impacting your work?

Implement what you've learned in this chapter and draft how you would open the conversation with your manager. As you compose your opening, keep the following questions in mind:

- ❏ Is your manager more task or relationship oriented?
- ❏ How comfortable are you in disclosing personal details?
- ❏ Will you need special accommodations or a change in schedule?
- ❏ What solution (or solutions) are you offering with the problem to mitigate the impact on your work?

CHAPTER 13

Taking Work and Life Head On

In your work life and your personal life, practice the principles of *Head On*. Follow the methods outlined in this book and do the exercises at the end of each chapter. Then practice some more. When you do, you'll find that it becomes easier and easier to address difficult situations as they arise. You may find that you had been spending hours ruminating about a situation that really only took a few minutes to resolve once you addressed it.

Your brain needs the practice in order for this process to become second nature. Remember that neurons that fire together wire together. Recall also that stressful situations will spike your cortisol and other stress hormone levels and, left unchecked, you will progress rapidly up the arousal continuum. Your brain falls back on what it knows best (this is why pilots train so extensively on what to do when things go wrong). Practice is the only way to get there.

DEVELOPING COMPETENCE

Don't expect perfection. You may stumble with mastering the skills and techniques outlined in this book. That's okay. It happens to all of us when we are learning a new skill. We move through four distinct stages as we gain mastery over a new skill. First, we are *unconsciously incompetent.* That is, we are not good at something and we don't even know it. It is in our blind spot, out of our conscious awareness. Then, something that happens that brings to our awareness this thing we didn't know we didn't know how to do. For example, you might go wind surfing for the first time. It looks easy enough. Who knew it would be so challenging? Perhaps it wasn't a good choice for a first date activity!

Once you reach this level of awareness, a level where you are sometimes painfully aware of your incompetence, you are *consciously incompetent.* You are bad at it and you know it. Maybe that's why you picked up this book.

Developing proficiency of a new skill requires that you take deliberate action to implement that new skill. Your cognitive load increases as you focus on each step of the new process, getting the steps in order and the timing right. You can do it, and you have to think about. At this point you are *consciously competent.*

Eventually, after you have successfully done something many, many times, it becomes second nature to you and you don't have to give it conscious thought—at least not the deliberate steps. You are *unconsciously competent.* You are good at it and you don't have to think about it to be good at it.

As you experiment, practice, and otherwise play around with the techniques shared in this book, you will move through the stages from unconscious incompetence to conscious and unconscious competence. When you've had hundreds of conversations on difficult and challenging topics and followed the steps outlined in this book, having those conversations will become an area of conscious competence for you, or perhaps even unconscious competence.

Remember to have compassion for yourself as you move through the stages. At first, you might see an opportunity three days later and think, "Oh, I could have used the Fact AND model!" Then, later another situation will occur and instead of three days, it will be three hours after the event that you realize the missed opportunity to use the technique.

As your confidence grows and the neural pathways that support these techniques develop and strengthen, you will get closer and closer to using the tools in the moment. At some point, you will be thinking about using one of the tools or techniques at the very time that you hear other words roll off your tongue and you will be wishing you could suck them back in. When that happens, stop. Take a breath. A deep breath. And begin again. You are getting there!

TAKING ACTION

Without action there is no change. If you read this book and implement none of it, you will be intellectually wiser. But your conversations on difficult topics will not be any easier. Strained relationships will not automatically improve. No, to make the principles in this book work for you, you need to put them to work.

This book is not a book with a few quick tips you can try or a silver bullet that will solve all of your difficult work situations and conversations. Rather, this is a book that suggests a fundamental shift in how you think about and approach difficult conversations. When you can keep in mind that other people don't like feeling threatened any more than you do, and that threats produce a natural, biological self-defense reaction, your approach to human interactions will be changed forever.

Understanding that the brain opts for defensive maneuvers and safety any time it feels threatened, and that it is biological, invariably changes things. You will be more mindful and deliberate with your word choices. You will work to create safe situations built on trust and respect. You will create conversations that are clear and free from emotional hazards.

And through the way you treat people and the example you set, you will change the world. You might not think you are changing it on a grand scale, but if you change the world for the better through your ability to successfully navigate a murky relationship with a coworker, that coworker's life will be better (and probably the lives of those around you, too).

Look for opportunities to change the world one conversation at a time. You might talk to your manager or your neighbor or your child differently. You might create a safe space in which to talk about salary disparity or racial justice or drug use. In opening up that discussion with that one person, you will change their world. For the better. And little by little, in conversations big and small, we will begin to create a world in which people listen to one another, respect one another, trust one another, and can take difficult situations head on.

Endnotes

1. Gallup Organization. (2013). "State of the American Workplace." http://www.gallup.com/services/178514/ state-american-workplace.aspx

2. Gibb, J.R. (1961). Defensive Communication. *Journal of Communication*, Vol. 11, pp. 141–148.

3. Stamp, G.H., A.L. Vangelisti and J.A. Daly. (1992). The creation of defensiveness in social interaction. *Communication Quarterly*, Vol. 40 (2).

4. Ramachandran, V.S. (2012). *The Tell-Tale Brain: A Neuroscientist's Quest for What Makes Us Human*. New York: Norton.

5. Caine, R.N., and G. Caine. (1994). *Making connections: teaching and the human brain*. Menlo Park, Calif: Addison-Wesley

6. Peng, B.D. (2006). Fear and Learning: Trauma-Related Factors in the Adult Education Process. In *The Neuroscience of Adult Learning*, Eds. Sandra Johnson and Kathleen Taylor, pp. 11-20.

7. Revelle, W. and D.A. Loftus. (1992). The Implications of Arousal Effects for the Study of Affect and Memory. In *The Handbook of Emotion and Memory*, pp. 113–150.

8. De Dreu, C. K.W.; M. Baas; and B.A. Nijstad. (2008). Hedonic tone and activation level in the mood-creativity link: Toward a dual pathway to creativity model. *Journal of Personality and Social Psychology*, Vol. 94(5), pp. 739-756.

9. Baer, M. and M. Frese. (2003). Innovation is not enough: climates for initiative and psychological safety, process innovations, and firm performance. *Journal of Organizational Behavior*, Vol. 24, pp. 45–68.

10. Edmondson, A. (1999). "Psychological Safety and Learning Behavior in Work Teams." *Administrative Science Quarterly*. 44 (2), pp. 350–383.

11. West, M.A. and N.R. Anderson. (1996). "Innovation in top management teams." *Journal of Applied Psychology*. 81 (6), pp. 680–693.

12. Carmeli, A., D. Brueller, and J.E. Dutton. (2009). Learning behaviours in the workplace: The role of high-quality interpersonal relationships and psychological safety. *Systems Research,* Vol. 26, pp. 81–98.

13. Nembhard, I.M., and A.C. Edmondson. (2006). Making it safe: the effects of leader inclusiveness and professional status on psychological safety and improvement efforts in health care teams. *Journal of Organizational Behavior*, Vol. 27, pp. 941–966.

14. Lambert, K. (2003). The life and career of Paul MacLean: a journey toward neurobiological and social harmony. *Physiology & Behavior*, 79, pp. 343-9.

15. Cronen, V.W., W.B. Pearce, and L.M. Snavely. (1979). A theory of rule-structure and types of episodes and a study of perceived enmeshment in undesired repetitive patterns. In D. Nimmo (Ed.), *Communication Yearbook*, Vol. 3, pp. 225-240. New Brunswick, NJ: Transaction Books.

16. Barsade, S. (2002). The Ripple Effect: Emotional Contagion and its Influence on Group Behavior. *Administrative Science Quarterly,* Vol. 47, pp. 644-675.

17. Ramachandran, V.S. (2012). *The Tell-Tale Brain: A Neuroscientist's Quest for What Makes Us Human.* New York: Norton.

18. Berger, C. R. and R.J. Calabrese. (1975). Some Explorations in Initial Interaction and Beyond: Toward a Developmental Theory of Interpersonal Communication. *Human Communication Research*, Vol. 1, pp. 99–112

19. Gordon, T. (1970). *P.E.T.: Parent Effectiveness Training.* New York: Harmony.

20. Bridges, W. (2004). *Transitions: Making Sense of Life's Changes*, 25th Ed. Boston: Da Capo Press.

21. Benitez-Quiroz, C.F., R. Wilbur, and A. Martinez. (2016). The not face: A grammaticalization of facial expressions of emotion. *Cognition*, Vol. 150, pp. 77–84.

22. Woolley, A.W., C.F. Chabris, A. Pentland, N. Hashmi, and T.W. Malone. (2010). Evidence for a collective intelligence factor in the performance of human groups. *Science*, 330, pp. 686-688.

23. Carnegie Mellon University. (2010). New Study by Carnegie Mellon, MIT and Union College Shows Collective Intelligence of Groups Exceeds Cognitive Abilities of Individual Group Members. Carnegie Mellon University | CMU. Retrieved from www.cmu.edu/news/archive/2010/October/oct1_collectiveintelligencestudy.shtml.

24. Littrell, J. (2015). *Neuroscience for Psychologists and Other Mental Health Professionals*. New York: Springer.

25. Olatunji, B.O., J.M. Lohr, and B.J. Bushman. (2007). The pseudopsychology of venting in the treatment of anger: Implications and alternatives for mental health practice. In T.Z. Cavell & K.T. Malcolm (Eds.), *Anger, aggression, and interventions for interpersonal violence*, pp. 119-141. Mahwah, NJ: Lawrence Erlbaum Associates.

26. Bastin, M., J. Vanhalst, R. Filip, and P. Bijttebier. (2017). Co-Brooding and Co-Reflection as Differential Predictors of Depressive Symptoms and Friendship Quality in Adolescents: Investigating the Moderating Role of Gender. *Journal of Youth and Adolescence*, pp. 1-15.

27. Saad, L. (2014). The "40-Hour" Workweek Is Actually Longer – by Seven Hours. Gallup News. Retrieved from http://news.gallup.com/poll/175286/hour-workweek-actually-longer-seven-hours.aspx.

28. Dweck, C. (2006). *Mindset: The New Psychology of Success*. New York: Ballantine.

Index

Acknowledgments

This book came to life through the assistance of many talented helpers. At Gale House Press, Tina's administrative skills pushed this project to the finish line on a cold winter day. I couldn't have done it without her. My editor, Camille Trentacoste, went above and beyond more times than I can count. Deep gratitude to Amy Jolin for (re)introducing me to Camille. Sheila Joyce deftly proofread the manuscript (over Thanksgiving weekend!). Special thanks also are due to Joey McGarvey who edited portions of an early draft of the book.

I am indebted to reviewers of the book proposal and early chapters: Pam Longfellow, Terri Cotts, and Erika Garms. They gave from their hearts and minds. I appreciate each of them for their belief in me and their unwavering friendship.

Special thanks go out to two very special people who offered up their homes to me as writing retreats at various points in the writing process: Heidi Palms and Kristen Kralick. Squirreling myself away from the duties of family and the busyness of my every-day life, in your apartment and your cabin respectively, was exactly what was needed to pull this off.

The writing process was made much more fun with the encouragement and inspiration of many of my fellow speaker/author friends, chief among them Theresa Rose and Kristen Brown.

I have deep gratitude for my parents. They believed in me, despite my sometimes unconventional choices, and their belief in me made a lasting difference.

And finally, I thank my family. The kids–Andrew, Jocelyn, and Blake–were an important part of the process. From helping out around the house, to creating a writing fairy to be my muse, to giving the best hugs ever, you continue to inspire me and make life more fun. And to Mark, my husband, who contributed more to this book than he knows. Thank you.

About the Author

Janel Anderson, PhD is a recognized expert on workplace communication and culture. She helps organizations untangle complex communication and relationship issues so employees and leaders alike can collaborate better and serve their customers more effectively.

Even more importantly, Anderson helps her clients develop new ways of relating to one another at work so they can get products to market faster, shorten sales cycles, and create value for their customers, all while recognizing their own humanity in the process.

Anderson holds a PhD in organizational communication from Purdue University. She has been a manager in a start-up company, a college professor, a director in a global organization, and in 2010 Anderson left her corporate role to found Working Conversations and hasn't looked back.

With clients like 3M, Wells Fargo, Cargill, Delta Dental, General Dynamics, Mayo Clinic, and Polaris, Anderson has helped notable brands improve their communication and culture. In addition, she's worked with hundreds of associations and government groups, sharing techniques on how to communicate more effectively at work.

For more information on speaking engagements, training programs, or workshops, please contact us at:

Janel Anderson
CEO & Founder
Working Conversations
P.O. Box 19453
Minneapolis, MN 55419
Phone: 612-327-8026
Email: janel@workingconversations.com
Website: WorkingConversations.com